Empowered Leadership

Workplace Wisdom for Aspiring Leaders

Chris Ellis

© 2020 by Chris Ellis

Edited by Grace Michael

Other books by Chris Ellis:

The Enlightened Enterprise
The Conscious and High Performing Organization

Light Your Path
Timeless Wisdom for Young People

Dedication

This book is dedicated to my clients.
I hope you have learned as much from me
as I have learned from you.

Acknowledgements

The author would like to thank the following people for their friendship, support, and faith:

Jeff Stoner, Tim Murray, John Marston,
Christopher Couillard, Mark Decker, Max Delgado,
Justin Diehl, and Jeff Shelstad

Contents

Contents v

Opening 1

Chapter 1 - The Foundations of Leadership 3

Chapter 2 - Strategy and Capability 25

Chapter 3 - Work, Networks, and Productivity 49

Chapter 4 - Culture and People 81

Chapter 5 - More Foundations of Leadership 103

Closing 127

Index 129

About the Author 131

Opening

In our digital age the nature of leadership is changing. A new generation of leaders must develop both timeless fundamentals and leading-edge abilities to face the many challenges and seize the many opportunities this era represents. This book will help you awaken to a new understanding of and readiness for what is required to be an empowered leader now and in the future.

While every generation shares similar needs, wants, and goals, each has unique characteristics as well. As an aspiring leader, you may have advanced quickly in your organization due in part to digital acumen and social media savvy. Chances are you work fast and like to multi-task. You have a lot of energy and are innovative, collaborative, and goal-oriented. You are well-educated, environmentally aware, and believe in social causes. You are cosmopolitan, thrive in multi-cultural settings, and expect progress to be big and bold and brisk.

Whether you are considered millennial, xennial, or other generation, there are likely traits that will challenge your leadership development and long-term success. Which of these questions resonate with you?

- To what extent are you relational or transactional? How intentional are you in building high quality relationships?
- How deeply do you understand external forces, internal systems, and the web of interactions that drive performance?
- To what extent do you have the attention span to plan, build, and sustain processes and networks? How patient are you?
- How well do you integrate work-life to manage stress and avoid burnout? How often do you unplug and recharge?
- To what extent do you define success as getting things done in the short-run versus making an impact in the long-run?

In this dynamic age of volatility, uncertainty, distraction, and velocity—with new business models and operating models and new ways of connecting, collaborating, and working—your leadership success will be determined by a commitment to lifelong learning, development, and renewal.

Along the way, you will need to develop greater depth and breadth of experiences through diverse projects and roles. You will need to shift from a *me* to a *we* orientation. And you will need to redefine conditioned concepts of power, impact, and success.

To get started, think about your experiences with and beliefs about leadership. Consider your strengths and weaknesses and their implications for new pathways of growth. Consider your perspective on these questions:

- What are the responsibilities of a leader? What are the competencies of a leader?
- What differentiates poor or mediocre leadership from good or great leadership?
- How can leaders improve focus, attention, and concentration in our age of distraction? Why should they?
- How can leaders build quality relationships in our age of transaction? Why should they?
- How can leaders achieve more impact and also harmonize work and life in ways that bring greater meaning?

This book will help you with the great paradox that you can slow down the busyness of work and life and speed up your growth as a leader. Much like life, leadership is a process of discovery. It is a lifelong project—with no real need to rush—that requires deep reflection, active engagement, and serious effort.

As you read this book, perhaps with a coach, colleague, or cohort, take comfort in knowing that leadership is learned and developed. You have the potential to become a great leader, make a lasting difference, and create an enduring legacy.

CHAPTER 1

Foundations of Leadership

If you want to be a leader, first learn to lead yourself. If you want to be a better leader, strive to become a better person.

Introduction

This chapter explores the foundations of leadership which include the building blocks of leadership effectiveness: the core responsibilities of leaders, the proven practices of good leaders, the competencies of enlightened leaders, and the wisdom pathways of self-actualized leaders.

Leadership has four key aspects: mindsets, behaviors, practices, and abilities. A leader's paradigm, or approach, or style, is most effective when these aspects are developed and applied in ways that are intentional, integral, inspirational, and impactful. Your paradigm will evolve as you grow as a leader. **See Diagram 1.**

In exploring this chapter, consider a few questions: What aspects of leadership are a strength that you will further develop? What aspects of leadership are a weakness that you will you begin to develop? What do you think it means to become more intentional, integral, inspirational, and impactful as a leader?

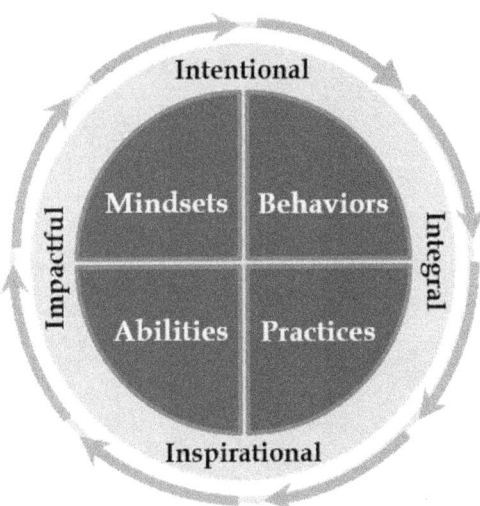

Diagram 1

Aspiring leaders are on a journey of self-actualization, a much more conscious level of participation in work and life with new ways of thinking, being, and doing.

Launching the Leadership Paradigm

Leadership is about who you are and who you can become. It is about what you do and how you engage others to get things done. Whether you are advancing in your organization, beginning a new job or career, or starting a new venture, effective leadership will likely be the single-most important key to your long-term success.

The organization of today and tomorrow is rapidly evolving. It is a networked entity with many types of leadership roles broadly distributed across loosely-defined structures. Leaders are not just at the top of the pyramid or at the center of the lattice; they lead the cooperation of people and achievement of results deep in the organization and on its outer edges. Work is influence-driven, highly fragmented, and very collaborative. New technologies continue to transform how people communicate, process information, and work together.

For these reasons the many forms and facets of leadership are evolving as well. Leaders lead processes, programs, projects, teams, functions, and organizations. They also lead emerging networks, virtual communities, and other webs of activity in new business models and the ecosystems in which they exist.

Leadership development is a top priority for most enterprises because of *both* its perceived importance *and* ineffectiveness. With this in mind, it is essential for the aspiring leader to take ownership for his or her own growth. This starts with creating a personal leadership approach, or paradigm.

The main elements of an individual's leadership paradigm are:

- **Mindsets**: Ways of thinking. The ways in which you think about yourself, the world, and your role as a leader. Your core beliefs, values, motivators, and frames—the mental models—that are both enabling *and* limiting, and that establish your attitudes, influence your behaviors, and guide your interactions with people. An example of a useful mindset is wanting to perform well as a leader not because of an anxious fear of failure but rather because of a healthy commitment to excellence.

- **Behaviors**: Ways of being. The ways in which you demonstrate your character and personality and show-up as a leader. Your modes of conduct in how you listen, react, speak, and relate to others. The ways in which you carry out your responsibilities and engage with and inspire people. An example of a useful behavior is an alert presence when interacting with others—how you listen actively and pay close attention without interrupting or getting distracted.

- **Practices**: Ways of working. The daily, weekly, and other periodic habits and routines you follow to be intentional and disciplined as a leader. The degree to which you establish useful activities that follow a consistent pattern and cadence, and that condition people in ways to help you engage them productively and effectively. An example of a good practice is a half-hour, mid-day meeting with self that is protected for contemplation, even meditation, to help flow with the day's situations, stay grounded, and stay focused on priorities.

- **Abilities**: Ways of doing. The breadth and depth of knowledge and subject matter expertise you apply in doing work. The core strengths you leverage and the related technical and interpersonal skills that enable you to be effective. This includes the key competencies of critical thinking, problem solving, and decision making. An example of a useful ability is influencing the decision-making process that affects funding and resource allocation for the team(s) you lead.

Helpful questions for getting started with a leadership paradigm include: What are some of my beliefs about myself and my experience and potential as a leader? What are my strengths? What feedback have I received along the way, both reinforcing and constructive? What personal and professional traits have enabled my success? What traits are potential limitations to future success? What challenges do I face over the next few years on my path? How will I seek guidance and ask for help?

The leadership paradigm develops over time as you evolve with leadership experience, perspective, and capability. We return to the concept of a paradigm at the end of this chapter.

Exploring the Role of Leadership

While the nature of leadership is evolving, the fundamentals of what leaders do on a daily basis are timeless. Basic leadership building-blocks are: asking questions, facilitating dialog, sharing information, delegating work, influencing others, making decisions, forging relationships, modeling norms, and building trust.

Building on these fundamentals, there are twelve core responsibilities of a leader (most of which require collaboration):

- *Managing self*: Management of one's attitude, attention, effort, and development.
- *Setting direction*: Development of strategies, imperatives, and priorities that define the desired path forward.
- *Allocating resources*: Optimal use of resources in supporting the prioritized needs of the organization.
- *Defining roles*: Design of organization structure and roles and jobs with clear responsibilities and expectations.
- *Aligning priorities*: Alignment of key priorities within and across organization functions and units.
- *Building teams*: Chartering, guidance, and support of formal and informal groups to drive strategy execution.
- *Coordinating activity*: Synchronization of work activity within and across organization functions and units.
- *Guiding processes*: Management and continuous improvement of business processes that drive results.
- *Inspiring people*: Creation of conditions that motivate and empower people to do their best work.
- *Developing talent*: Commitment to personal and professional learning, development, and growth of people.
- *Driving results*: Focus, urgency, and determination in achieving superior results over the long-term.
- *Shaping culture*: Role-modeling core values, behaviors, and cultural norms in daily interactions.

In carrying out these core responsibilities, leaders can apply a rubric of success that represents the diversity of stakeholders involved. In this sense, leadership impact is stakeholder impact. Types of stakeholder impact include impact on customer, self, team, function, enterprise, owner, and community.

Impact is often defined in terms of what was achieved and how it was achieved relative to expectations, standards, goals, or performance ranges. Impact reflects both qualitative outcomes and quantitative results relating to the triple-bottom line: economic, social, and environmental value.

Leadership is a continuous learning process, the art and science of becoming. Learning to be a good leader goes hand-in-glove with developing as a good person—learning how to do the right thing for the right reasons in the right ways. Thus, leadership starts with two simple truths: **If you want to be a leader, first learn to lead yourself. If you want to be a better leader, strive to become a better person.**

Building on the core responsibilities and simple truths, there are twelve proven practices of good leadership:

- *Leaders generate positive energy and hope about the future.* They unite people around an inspiring mission and vision.
- *Leaders consistently define and communicate clear priorities.* They emphasize clarity, focus, and alignment.
- *Leaders build great teams.* They develop unified, capable, and empowered groups of people.
- *Leaders know the business and reinforce reality.* They challenge people with a shared responsibility for the truth.
- *Leaders demonstrate a growth mindset.* They embrace both fear and failure as fuel for continuous learning.
- *Leaders emphasize strategy, culture, and people.* They create the conditions for people to do their best work.
- *Leaders make decisions, direct attention, and align resources.* They direct resources and talent to where they most need to go.

Chapter 1 - Foundation of Leadership

- *Leaders play the long game.* They balance the short- and long-term and coevolve with the external ecosystem.
- *Leaders relentlessly focus on improving results.* They constantly optimize cost, quality, productivity, and service.
- *Leaders attract, develop, and retain the right people.* They use performance management as a key business process.
- *Leaders are authentic, ethical, and trustworthy.* They are open, transparent, vulnerable, receptive, and consistent.
- *Leaders live a personal mission and are fit in mind, body, spirit.* They model good values and habits but do not try to be heroes.

One way to assess progress in developing leadership capability is to measure the impact on stakeholders. With respect to the leader's team(s), good impact questions to explore include: Are people inspired and engaged? Are they focused and productive? Are they supported and learning? Are they recognized and rewarded? Are the best people staying? And, are they doing their best work?

With core responsibilities and proven practices, we have made a good start in exploring effective leadership. Next we explore the use of competencies.

Elevating Leadership Competencies

Competencies are powerful tools in leadership development. Leadership competency models should meet several criteria. They align with the drivers of strategy execution, link to the core capabilities of the organization, reinforce the desired culture and value system of the enterprise, and reflect the distinctive abilities of exemplar leaders who are more effective than others.

Leadership competency models seek to combine into bundles the skills, knowledge and abilities for a) strategic, business, technical, and digital acumen, with b) how to influence, engage, and enable people to do their best work. In our age of disruptive business models, complex networked organizations, and volatile business ecosystems, the definition of "leader" is transforming and a model of more enlightened leadership is needed.

Building on emotional intelligence, leadership agility, and other relevant frameworks, the competencies of wise and enlightened leadership can enhance a standard management competency model that may already be in place.

Twelve competencies of enlightened leadership are:

- *Self-awareness*: Regulating emotion and ego-driven thinking and doing, paying close attention to the mind's pervasive cognitive distortions, defense mechanisms, and conditioned biases, and how these affect interactions with others.

- *Practical mindfulness*: Demonstrating an objective awareness of and attention to the present moment with a detached processing of external stimuli and without judging, filtering, or assigning emotional meaning to them.

- *Situational agility*: Integrating and applying learnings from experience to new and dynamic challenges, and navigating difficult situations constructively to achieve specific goals and desirable outcomes.

- *Evaluative clarity*: Understanding the difference between observation that yields objective points of data with assessment that yields subjective points of view.

- *Appreciative curiosity*: Valuing differences in diverse ideas and perceptions of the past and present when vibrantly exploring questions about change for the future.

- *Persuasive listening*: Seeking to understand, probing through insightful questions, and being careful of obstacles to active listening, such as mindreading, sparring, and placating.

- *Systems seeing*: Perceiving the specific opportunity or challenge in relation to the whole set of moving and relevant parts, and how they are integrated with and influence one another in driving total system outcomes.

- *Proper altitude*: Framing work at the right level of abstraction, and operating in the middle of the delegation continuum, avoiding "go figure it out" hands-off abdication and "let's get it done right now" hands-on control.

- *Careful discernment*: Applying critical thinking to efficiently make astute decisions in a manner that is rational and informed by facts, but without expensive and unnecessary data and analytics.

- *Pragmatic optimism*: Integrating idealistic values with hard-boiled realities of how complex problems are solved when there are diverse stakeholders and competing interests.

- *Comfortable equanimity*: Accepting any situation or circumstance as a natural state, without resistance, and embracing uncertainty with a calm poise and open mind.

- *Sincere empathy*: Demonstrating a respect and compassion for the physical, emotional, mental, and spiritual well-being of people, and an understanding of how personal challenges can affect performance.

Becoming a leader is a process of broadening perspective, expanding awareness, and developing wisdom. Enlightened leaders fluidly navigate organizational power structures, collaborate across silos and boundaries, and replace their personal agenda with the mission of the enterprise. They ask a lot of questions, thrive on feedback, explore new ideas, cultivate new mindsets.

In today's dynamic landscape, standard talent development processes need to be augmented with the competencies of more empowered and impactful leadership. Leaders can enhance their development by including one or more of these in each cycle of their growth plan.

Playing Your A-Game of Actualization

Building on enlightened competencies, a more in-depth examination of leadership wisdom is worthwhile. Having fun with alliteration, we can explore an A-framework of self-actualization.

Use this A-frame to play your A-game for greater impact:

- **Awareness.** In the context of leadership, awareness begins with self-awareness and reflects a clear sense of reality and one's self in the world. In the dynamic energy field of existence, the leader monitors and manages his or her beliefs and perceptions to gain greater insight into how the world works.

Almost all activity occurs in relational, systemic, and interdependent webs of activity. Awareness requires an alertness to the present moment with a panoramic view. It is widening the aperture to see systems and recognize patterns, notice what is there and not there, and be open to the many perspectives of diverse stakeholders. Very important, it is also an understanding of how we are conditioned by beliefs and forces that do not always serve us or others very well.

Consider how a new leader immersed the team in studying the moment-by-moment dynamics in distribution channels, and as a result, better harmonized interactions with channel partners to grow revenue.

With respect to awareness, the aspiring leader evolves in emphasis from a *me* orientation and *seeking approval* to that of a *we* orientation and *serving others*.

- **Attention.** In the context of leadership, attention reflects the power of mindful focus and concentration on what matters most. The plague in most organizations today is that of attention deficit and disorder: frantic and fragmented work activity, constant distractions and interruptions, and ineffective and costly multi-tasking. Attention requires discipline in prioritizing work, balancing urgent and important activities, communicating clearly, and collaborating fully. Attention reflects perhaps the most fundamental law of management: *It is never about time and always about priority.*

Consider how a new leader implemented new protocols for communicating and collaborating in ways that increased total productivity *and* reduced workload at the same time.

With respect to attention, the aspiring leader evolves in emphasis from the *volume* of completing work activities to the *impact* of achieving key priorities.

- **Attitude.** In the context of leadership, attitude reflects the positive optimism required in an often upside-down world. A positive attitude means keeping things in a balanced perspective and not allowing limiting beliefs, dark forces, or negative self-talk to get in the way of doing the right thing. Attitude involves adapting and responding to situations in bold, resilient, joyful, and hopeful ways. It requires understanding the nature of fear and learning from failure. And it involves a commitment to serving and empowering others.

Consider how a new leader navigated a steep learning curve by reframing every difficult situation in real-time as exactly what was needed — in the spirit of acceptance and gratitude.

With respect to attitude, the aspiring leader evolves in emphasis from a tendency toward *limitation* and *scarcity* to that of *opportunity* and *growth*.

- **Aptitude.** In the context of leadership, aptitude reflects the depth and breadth of abilities needed to manage work and lead people. Critical acumens include emotional intelligence, business intelligence, and cultural intelligence. Key competencies are critical thinking, problem solving, and decision making. Both social and technical skills are essential. Aptitude involves the concurrent development of leadership ability, functional excellence, and job-mastery.

  Consider how a new leader further enhanced digital acumen of the business unit by adopting a new cognitive technology to facilitate better team-based problem-solving.

  With respect to aptitude, the aspiring leader evolves from *doing* and delivering to *delegating* and coordinating to *directing* and encouraging.

- **Agency.** In the context of leadership, agency is influencing others to drive results in meaningful ways without overusing role-based authority. Natural power, or authentic power, is a function of principle, purpose, passion, preparation, proficiency, patience, perseverance, and performance. These sources of power enable the leader guide activities and get stuff done without command and control behavior. Agency comes from how the leader listens, speaks, and acts in a manner that establishes respect, builds trust, and inspires effort.

  Consider how a new leader relentlessly communicated three key priorities across the function, encouraged staff to try new approaches and make mistakes, and used cross-team forums to openly debrief failures and celebrate learnings.

With respect to agency, the aspiring leader evolves from an artificial and transactional use of *force* to an authentic and relational use of *power*.

- **Alignment.** In the context of leadership, alignment reflects the coordination of priorities, plans, processes, projects, and people. This includes aligning work activities and allocating resources across functions to break down silos and drive total system performance. Synchronizing strategy execution, alignment reduces waste and inefficiency and increases speed and productivity across boundaries.

  Consider how a new leader implemented dynamic resource allocation process to frequently review the status of key priorities and initiatives and reallocate resources in real-time.

  With respect to alignment, the aspiring leader evolves from *resource maximization* within a group to that of *resource optimization* across groups.

- **Altitude.** In the context of leadership, altitude reflects the ability to operate at the right place on the strategic vs tactical spectrum given the needs of the situation and audience. Right altitude involves real-time discernment about the role of the leader in a situation and how to best align, coordinate, guide, and drive activity to achieve results. This entails avoiding the unhelpful extremes of macromanaging hands-off abdication and micromanaging hands-on control.

  Consider how a new leader gained support from senior leaders for a new initiative by precisely connecting improvements in service quality for ideal customers with the potential for growth in an underdeveloped market.

  With respect to altitude, the aspiring leader evolves in emphasis from *executing* tasks to *implementing* programs to *guiding* strategies, and fluidly navigates across all three.

- **Amplitude.** In the context of leadership, amplitude reflects the degree to which the leader's emotions are managed and adjusted in the moment. Emotional regulation is achieved through low variance in behavior and a calm go-with-the-flow composure regardless of circumstances. A natural intensity is demonstrated in all situations as productive vitality rather than as disruptive volatility.

Consider how a new leader refused to bite-the-hook in tough meetings through the practice of pause-and-effect: refraining from reacting with emotion and reframing as an opportunity to be helpful.

With respect to amplitude, the aspiring leader evolves from a common state of excitability to that of equanimity in challenging and stressful situations.

- **Accountability.** In the context of leadership, accountability reflects the initiative and ownership needed for achieving results. It is a proactive rather than reactive posture that involves clearly assessing the nature of an opportunity or problem, defining desired results or impact, aligning around a solution or strategy, and engaging others to execute a plan with discipline. It is a see-it, own-it, solve-it, do-it approach.

  Consider how a new leader used a diagnostic tool with the team for isolating weak-links in processes, rather than breakdowns in job performance, as an early focus for improving results — a blame the process not the person approach.

  With respect to accountability the aspiring leader evolves in emphasis from doing the job (responsibility) to that of achieving the results (accountability).

- **Agility.** In the context of leadership, agility reflects making decisions, taking action, and leading others in highly dynamic situations and in real-time. Agility is anticipating change, seeing systems, recognizing patterns, and reading situations to rapidly reframe and readjust as needed. It is a willingness to try new approaches as new conditions or challenges arise. Agility is making small moves and incremental changes that build on each other to persistently navigate in the direction of desired results.

  Consider how a new leader openly acknowledged the need to learn in real-time how to implement new regulations, leading the function to monitor all moving parts and make small daily adjustments to ensure long-term success.

> With respect to agility, the aspiring leader evolves from *reacting* impulsively to *responding* thoughtfully to what people say and do.

Perhaps there is another A-frame for playing your A-game. This is the frame of **Actualization** itself. Aspiring leaders are on a journey of self-actualization: the development of a much more conscious level of participation as a leading contributor that requires more mindful ways of being and doing.

Self-actualization comes from self-awareness, self-acceptance, and self-improvement. But it is not self-absorption. Actualization enables the leader to be humble but also confident, focused but also flexible, assertive but also collaborative, and passionate but also composed in working with and leading others.

Integrating the Elements of Leadership

High performing professionals who are accelerating into formal leadership roles consistently demonstrate the humility to keep learning; the courage to try new things; the boldness to suggest new ideas; the confidence to ask for help; the kindness to empathize with others; and the commitment to always perform at their best. *To what extent do these characteristics describe you?*

Aspiring leaders are evolving from a competitive to a cooperative energy field, from an emphasis on individual achievement to that of collaborative results, and from delivering work to empowering others. These paradigms involve creating new mindsets, behaviors, practices, and abilities—that is, new ways of thinking, being, doing, and working. *To what extent do these paradigm elements resonate with your own ideas about growth?*

There is a lack of trust in our institutions today and a lack of integrity among many of our leaders. What an opportunity for a new generation of leaders to fill the void and usher in a new era of enterprise value creation where people in organizations are doing the right things in the right ways for the right reasons. *To what extent do your actions reflect respect, trust, and integrity?*

Leaders who are considered trustworthy, and who create climates of trust, demonstrate several behaviors and practices. First, they are honest. They do not lie or omit information on purpose. They do not minimize or magnify reality. They are candid but also kind. They do not horde information and are willing to share information with others. They are open and receptive to new ideas they may not agree with or did not originate. They ask people for feedback, are sincerely interested in acting on that feedback, and close the loop with people on why or why not action was taken. They are consistent, reliable, and mostly predictable in their behaviors, and these behaviors are composed and deliberate rather than careless and impulsive. And they are respected — but not always liked — because they treat others with kindness, respect, and dignity.

Like trust, enterprise integrity begins with leadership integrity: the degree to which leaders develop, integrate, and apply the mindsets, behaviors, practices, and abilities of good leadership. We will now return to the four leadership paradigm strategies of intentional, integral, inspirational, and impactful:

- **Intentional**. The leader acts with clear purpose and focused attention in developing specific mindsets, behaviors, practices, and abilities. The leader is highly deliberate in demonstrating his or her leadership style. An example of intentional leadership is the leader who, after receiving feedback that he was acting arrogantly in meetings, changed the nature of his participation from needing to be right to wanting to be helpful. He was very purposeful about asking one or two questions when engaging in the discussion and connecting ideas to make steady progress rather than giving answers to get quick results. *Are you being more intentional in your leadership approach and development?*

- **Integral**. The leader integrates beliefs, values, strengths, and limitations to lead others as an authentic, self-actualized human who is humble, open, and approachable. The leader aligns priorities and balances work through a disciplined cadence in management practices and coherence in leadership behaviors. An example of integral leadership is the leader who held a team meeting every week with a standing agenda that always involved solving a problem or making a decision. She included an agenda item where she role-modeled discussing a time management problem that she was dealing with herself, showing vulnerability, seeking input on potential solutions, and asking others to share their own challenges as well. *Are you integrating the key aspects of leadership along with work-life in meaningful ways?*

- **Inspirational.** The leader communicates a motivating vision for the future and exudes a hopeful energy. The leader encourages creativity and experimentation, involves people in determining how work gets done, and engages them in making decisions. The leader role-models a spirit of constant learning and continuous improvement. An example of inspirational leadership is the leader who recognized his people frequently in informal conversations when they demonstrated a specific value of the enterprise in their work. And he connected how he believed the demonstrated value increased their contribution to results. *Are you building trust while demonstrating a consistently positive attitude?*

- **Impactful.** The leader realizes greater satisfaction, meaning, and fulfillment through new levels of leadership ability. The leader makes a greater contribution to key results by leading others to do their best. An example of impactful leadership is the new leader who reframed her concept of success as helping her direct reports, many of who were new to their role as well, develop their own growth plans for long-term success at the expense of short-term gains. *Are you increasing your breadth of impact as you develop in your role?*

Leaders who sustain a steep growth curve into higher impact roles are very active, but don't overdo it, and take time to relax and recharge. There is a rhythm to daily life that feels good and that is nourishing mentally, physically, and emotionally. There is a commitment to fitness in mind, body, and spirit.

To develop high-performance habits, aspiring leaders are well-served to consider the four legs of the integrated work-life stool: family and friends; health and wellness; work and career; and interests and pursuits. The sustainable leader has learned to manage this stool where busyness and burnout are avoided, and one or more legs are rarely out-of-balance for very long.
See Diagram 2.

Chapter 1 - Foundation of Leadership

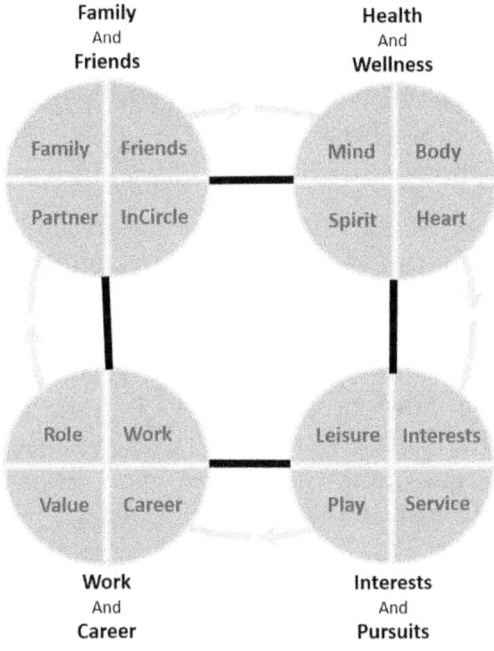

Diagram 2

Flowing in the Dynamic Energy Field

Equanimity is welcoming every situation as an opportunity to learn and serve. It is a calm, composed, and dignified attitude of appreciating each life experience. It is an alert awareness and attention that enables leaders to better flow with and navigate the daily shifting terrain.

Matthew Crawford, the social scientist, has said, "We live in an age of distraction that requires a new ethics of attention." Herbert Simon, the economist and psychologist, has said, "A wealth of information creates a poverty of attention."

What do focusing attention and going-with-the flow have to do with being a leader and developing your leadership approach? Both relate to the importance of slowing down right now to speed up later in leading your team, function, or organization for both short-term results and longer-term success.

Empowered Leadership

Existence in our shared energy field is not a discrete function. Leadership of self and others is a continuous flow experience. While we perceive life and work as event-driven—with workouts, meetings, appointments, dinners, etc.—much of our experience unfolds in the in-between. As Pema Chodron, the spiritual wisdom teacher has said, "Our path is the moment-by-moment unfolding of experience in a dynamic world."

We tend to think of our experience as chunked into the activities of leaving, arriving, and attending events, often with unwanted waiting involved, where we get frustrated and impatient and squeeze-in a bunch of busy work to get things done if we can. It might seem that multi-tasking is productive and constant motion is necessary, but how conscious are we in these moments? How intentional? In the in-between, how might you be more focused rather than fragmented? How might you become more discerning rather than distracted?

There are two types of in-between: scheduled and unscheduled. An example of scheduled is blocking time on the calendar for catching up. An example of unscheduled is traveling from one meeting to the next. Leaders who pay attention to the in-between look for better ways to be less busy and more intentional, inspirational, and impactful in the flowing river of the day.

For example, rather than constantly checking messages or newsfeeds, leaders might reflect on how well they are managing up, managing across, and managing down. Consider the new head of client service at a major law firm who, several times a day, would use his "free time" not to respond to emails but to proactively build good relationships in a focused manner. He might check-in with a partner-boss to discuss a strategic issue (managing up), connect with a peer to offer help on a key initiative (managing across), or engage with his team leaders to assist in removing an obstacle to progress (managing down).

In both life and work, we are conditioned to be "always-on" where we are constantly accessible and interruptible, checking messages, getting pulled into conversations, and firing off responses or requests, sometimes in the space of a few minutes or seconds. This constant partial attention is an epidemic among leaders and conditions others to work the same way. Instead, leaders can give full attention to the in-between, not to get more work done, but to do more important work differently. This is a great practice for becoming less automatic and more intentional, shifting the balance from false urgency to real value.

In the continuous flow of daily experience, leaders understand everything is a process that is guided and not controlled. Consider the leader of an analytics group in a commercial real-estate firm who was very frustrated with the monthly financial review meeting with senior leaders. Each month she prepared extensively for every possible question or potential issue, and each month the meeting would go sideways on what she perceived to be unimportant items not on the agenda. She viewed the monthly meeting as a discrete event "to get ready for" and was always disappointed. Once she recognized the true purpose of the meeting—to give senior leaders the opportunity to share input in a formal setting—she prepared for the meeting, participated in the dialog, and processed its outcomes differently and more effectively. She found a way to flow in a more relaxed way and make the in-between much more value-adding. She reframed the monthly cycle as an ongoing opportunity to learn.

With a continuous flow orientation, leaders can be more intentional in planting seeds and pulling weeds for improvement. They can make small moves that make a big difference. While the formal presentation, with all of its bells and whistles, is necessary and important, the informal conversations before and after with the right people can be even more impactful.

In the spirit of flowing with equanimity and making small moves, the leader of a start-up decided he needed to change certain behaviors and practices in informal interactions. He stopped talking so much and started asking more questions. And he stopped responding immediately to most emails and started calling three people (or stopping by their office) each day to have a meaningful conversation about key priorities.

Leaders stay present in the moment. They set direction, trust people to do their best, allow them to make mistakes, and candidly follow-up to share learnings. They invest in the well-being of themselves and others. They take the time to build high quality relationships with their teams, their colleagues, and often with their customers. They do not impulsively react to difficult circumstances, and stay calm and positive. They look for pivotal moments—both public and private—to demonstrate key values and show resilience in the face of constant change. They show up as leaders at formal events *and* in the in-between moments.

Leaders know that failure happens, and they accept it, learn from it, and reinforce this mindset with their teams as well. They are open-minded, adaptable, proactive, and keep things in proper perspective. They do not wait for change to happen to them and do not back-down from hard decisions. They are humble but also confident, and patient but also tenacious. Leaders lead themselves first. They are disciplined about healthy balance in their life, and how their responsibilities, activities, and experiences can blend together in work-life harmony.

Let's return to the paradigm elements. Consider the following questions to start thinking about and developing your own leadership paradigm (which is further explored in Chapter 5):

- What do you believe about people? What do you believe about leadership? What is your definition of leadership?

- What do you believe about yourself? What have been your leadership experiences as a leader and with other leaders?

- What are your leadership strengths and needs? How might you learn more about what these are?

- What do you believe about time, impact, and success? How might you measure progress in new ways?

- What new mindsets, behaviors, practices, and abilities might you focus on to grow as a leader?

- How can you become more intentional, integral, inspirational, and impactful as a leader?

CHAPTER 2
Strategy and Capability

Strategy defines the future direction of the enterprise and how it will win in the marketplace through competitive advantage. It is an ongoing process of creative problem solving to meet a need in a competitively superior way.

Chapter 2 - Strategy and Capability

Introduction

This chapter explores the fundamentals of strategy and capability. It focuses on customer acquisition, strategic framework definitions, value generating activities, strategy map creation, strategic entrepreneurship, and strategy execution as integral to the transformation required in our changing world.

As you read and think about this chapter, consider how your impact as a leader is linked to your effectiveness in setting direction, developing strategy, and creating the conditions for your team(s) to execute strategy and achieve results. Consider how strategy must evolve with the external environment.

In exploring this chapter, consider a few questions: What aspects of strategy and capability will you strengthen or begin developing at this stage in your growth as a leader? What mindsets, behaviors, practices, and abilities are needed? What topics would you like to study further to deepen your understanding?

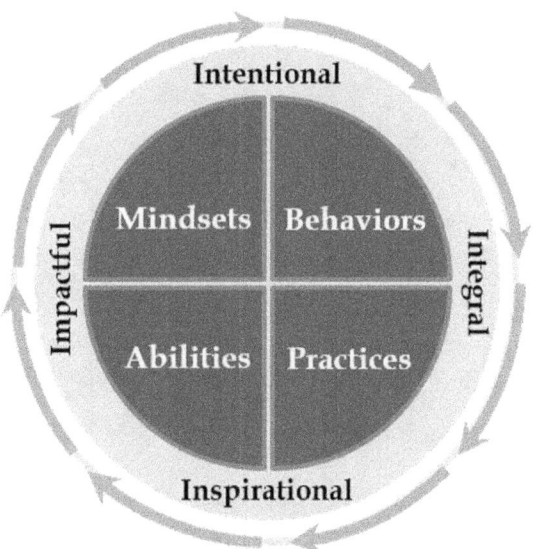

Diagram 1

Capabilities drive all value creation over the long-term. They are value-generating bundles of activity that require cross-functional enterprise synergy.

A fundamental truth is that these capabilities will always fall into one of four value creation bundles: innovation, generation, operation, or transaction.

Increasing Strategic Focus on Customers

A common challenge today is insufficient attention to the most important element of strategy: finding, getting, and keeping customers to drive profitable growth. Many organizations—in both the for-profit and non-profit sectors—do not focus enough on how to best grow their customer base or efficiently pursue their ideal, most profitable customers. In the non-profit world, profitable growth can be viewed as financially sound growth.

An effective approach to increasing customer focus when scaling-up or driving growth requires both disciplined thinking in strategic planning and aligned action in strategy execution.

While organizations often do not perceive themselves as short-changing customer acquisition, it is easy to do. It may even seem warranted, with the ever-present range of activity that demands leadership mindshare, such as a new cloud application, an ERP installation, or a fundraising or recapitalization initiative. Consider the medical device company that focused significant strategic planning attention on future revenue growth areas, but when it came to execution, it emphasized supply chain transformation to simplify its product portfolio and improve margins. And it did so at the expense of finding new customers and growing current customer share. There was much attention to profitable growth in its strategic planning work, but this did not translate into a well-resourced, top-priority, or commercially-integrated customer acquisition initiative.

Strategy involves setting direction, prioritizing activity, aligning functions, allocating resources, engaging people, and driving execution. It is developed within a three-dimensional space of 1) products and services; 2) markets, channels, and customers; and 3) processes and capabilities. This is also known as the M^3 framework of model, market, and management.

There are many helpful strategic models used in organizations today. The old standbys remain very good at helping identify potential markets, clarify points of differentiation, and solidify competitive advantage.

For example, Porter's model suggests an emphasis on one or at most two of three main *strategic choices*: cost leadership, product and service differentiation, or target market focus. Tracey's model suggests an emphasis on one or at-most two of three main *strategic capabilities*: operational excellence, customer intimacy, or product and service innovation.

There is a third model that organizations have found helpful in linking strategic planning and execution with a strong emphasis on customer acquisition and revenue growth. This model suggests one or at-most two of three *strategic intents*: set the pace (agility), change the rules (influence), or see the future (insight).

In all three models it is important to note the concept avoiding the "mush" of the middle. Strategy is about choice, and leaders and their teams must make decisions and place bets in defining a focused path forward. Strategies must evolve but focus remains critical. **See Diagram 3.**

Setting the pace reflects the strategic intent of *agile execution*, where the enterprise wins in the marketplace by going head-to-head with competitors in the arena of speed and change. Consider the agribusiness company that implemented commercial teams — integrated sales, marketing, and operations teams — to adapt and outperform competitors to gain share in the industry's consolidating distributor network.

Changing the rules reflects the strategic intent of *influence*, where the enterprise wins in the marketplace by changing the way business is done and how customers are won. Consider the for-profit education company that collaborated with regulators and quality assurance agencies to develop industry standards that created customer advantage in a highly competitive space.

Seeing the future reflects the strategic intent of *insight*, where the enterprise wins in the marketplace by consistently seeing beyond the horizon of the current landscape. Consider the behavioral health non-profit start-up that identified an intersection of socio-economic forces where a very large and growing group of underserved clients resided.

Chapter 2 - Strategy and Capability

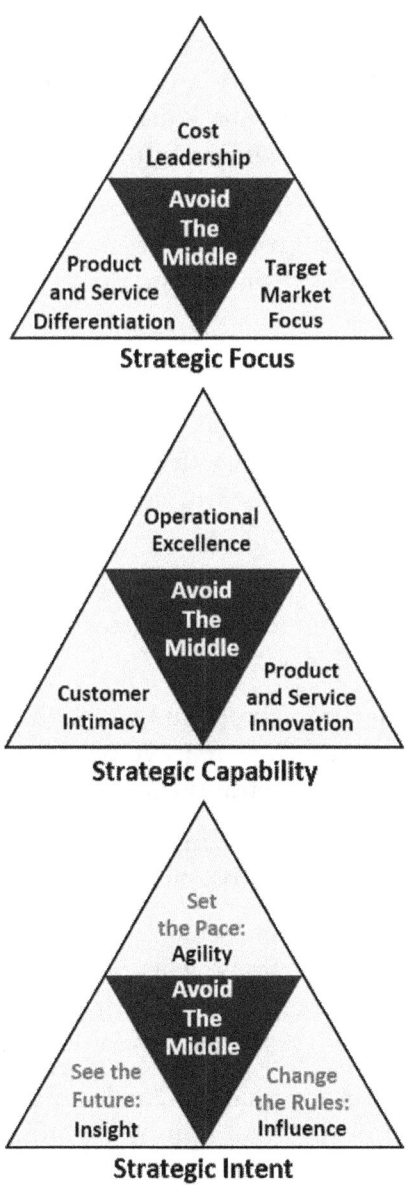

Diagram 3

Strategic planning and execution are not separate activities, but rather elements along a continuum, *especially* with regard to acquiring and serving customers. There are several questions leaders can explore to ensure a customer-centric strategy and operating plan (please note these need to be considered in terms of both the current and emerging future state):

- How does the enterprise acquire, serve, grow, and retain customers? What is the go-to-market strategy? What is the customer acquisition model and program?

- How are customers segmented? How are ideal customers defined, segmented, and targeted?

- How well is the organization performing relative to its customer acquisition and growth goals? How well is the value proposition of products and services attracting customers and meeting their needs?

- What is the cost of customer acquisition? What is the profit per customer? What are the key cost and revenue drivers? How do these differ by segment?

- Has the organization completed a fact-based SWOT analysis for customer acquisition, market penetration and development, and channel penetration and development?

- How does the enterprise win in the marketplace and what mix of capabilities and processes are required to do this?

- How does the customer-focused strategy translate into commercial-driven operations? Has the strategy been mapped for all functions to ensure that customer-focused activity is prioritized, aligned, resourced, and integrated?

- How well do metrics, analytics, and incentives support effective and efficient customer acquisition and growth?

- To what extent is there a systematic approach for learning, capability-building, and continuous improvement that is focused on customer acquisition and growth?

Chapter 2 - Strategy and Capability

- With respect to all of these questions: How will the enterprise need to evolve over the near-term, intermediate-term, and long-term scenarios to achieve profitable growth?

A successful, non-profit consumer research institute, confronted with new substitutes for its services, explored these questions in its strategic planning process and developed a customer-focused strategy map. Integral to *service differentiation* and *target market focus* as its competitive advantage was the strategic intent of *changing the rules*.

With two distinct types of customers—consumer products clients doing research, and the consumer product testers themselves—the institute defined three of the four strategic imperatives as critical to customer acquisition.

These included reprioritizing outreach efforts to pursue new and targeted prospects, reallocating resources to more efficiently reach ideal customers, and rebuilding better relationships with buying customers and their influential upstream colleagues (who determined research budgets) and with whom the organization historically had little contact.

Using its first-ever strategy map, it deployed cross-functional strategy execution teams, mobilizing people to prioritize their efforts on the most fundamental goal of achieving healthy financial growth through better customer acquisition, retention, and growth. Leaders implemented a non-traditional approach to performance management to drive strategy execution: the process was repurposed to center on a monthly review of both functional and cross-functional teams' milestone-based, customer-driven priorities and activities.

Increasing the emphasis on customer-focused strategy execution requires an enterprise to take a more attentive, disciplined, and rigorous approach to not just the "what" but also the "how" of finding, getting, and keeping customers to grow revenue and profit. And success is ultimately determined by the degree to which people at all levels are engaged, enabled, and incented across functions to efficiently acquire and effectively serve these customers.

Defining the Business Model and Strategy

Setting direction is a core responsibility of leadership. Leaders are often involved in developing and implementing a path forward, and thus need good working definitions of both business model and strategy, which are often conflated.

The *business model* describes the logic framework for how the enterprise creates value. The business model defines how the pieces of the business come together to convert the value proposition into value creation using capabilities. It reflects how a firm generates revenue, manages expenses, and makes a profit. It explains the services the firm plans to market, sell, and deliver. Popular business models are peer-to-peer (Airbnb), freemium (Spotify), subscription (Netflix), and franchising (Orangetheory). Deloitte found that only 30-percent of organizations believe they have the leadership skills to execute their evolving model.

The *strategy* defines future direction of the enterprise and how it will win in the marketplace through competitive advantage. It reflects the intersection of an organization's internal resources and capabilities and its external risks and opportunities. It is an ongoing process of creative problem solving to meet a need or set of needs in a competitively superior way.

A good strategy is clear, focused, distinctive, compelling, and balanced. A robust strategy can have multiple strategic goals, imperatives, and time horizons, and is not set in stone: it changes and evolves as guided by the leaders of the enterprise.

Several good strategic questions for a leadership team include:

- What is our mission—What business are we in and why? What is our vision of success in the short- and long-term?
- What is our business model—How will we make money? What are the key markets, channels, revenue streams, costs, and drivers of profitability?
- What is our external value proposition—How will we differentiate and win in the marketplace?
- What are our strategic and core capabilities—What are our sources of competitive advantage?

- What is our strategy — What is our path forward with respect to innovation, customer acquisition, revenue generation, and service operations?
- What is our operating model — How will we make, deliver, and support our services to deliver value to customers and create value for the enterprise?
- What is our culture — What values and norms are critical for us? What is our employee value proposition?

The capabilities of an enterprise make the difference between success and failure. An enterprise capability is a bundle of tangible and intangible activities for doing work and creating value. It often reflects a combination of process, people, and technology. It is the systemic integration of practices, competencies, and resources, and is often seen as the secret sauce to sustained excellence. Capability is dependent on key interactions of communication, coordination, and collaboration throughout the organization. **It is important to note that leadership may be the most important capability in any enterprise — the degree to which there are diverse and capable leaders throughout the organization.**

There are three capability types that are helpful to distinguish:

- **Strategic capability** is about leading the marketplace with what the enterprise is best at. Strategic capability in a clinic with specialized services, such as chronic pain, might be *care management*: forecasting, scheduling, coordinating, and treating patients.
- **Core capability** is about delivering the brand promise with what the enterprise is really good at. Core capability in the chronic pain clinic might be *program management*: developing, delivering, and managing the lifecycle of patient care programs.
- **Threshold capability** is about keeping the lights on and reflects what the enterprise is just good enough at. Threshold capability in the chronic pain clinic might be *compliance management*: meeting clinical, regulatory, and other agency requirements.

Strategic and core capabilities drive all value creation over the long-term. They can be described as value-generating bundles of activity that require cross-functional enterprise synergy. A fundamental truth is that strategic and core capabilities will *always* fall into one of four value creation bundles:

- **Innovation: creating and commercializing new products and services.** At a start-up educational services company, going-to-market with new and expanded services to support the core learning technology was critical to drive growth.

- **Generation: developing and growing markets, channels, and customers.** It was imperative for the company to develop a network of early adopters, master-trainers, and brand ambassadors to generate revenue.

- **Operation: making, delivering, and supporting products and services.** At the same company, a key priority was building a highly interactive e-commerce site with full functionality for customers, trainers, and partners.

- **Transaction: initiating and guiding mergers, acquisitions, and integrations.** The same company acquired a small struggling firm with complementary software, services, and sales channels, and continued to explore new mergers.

Today leaders invest too much attention and resources on the transaction activity of value to drive fast inorganic growth, and too little on the other three activities that drive sustainable organic growth. This is a main reason why the lifespans of many firms are short: leaders are not effectively building sustainable organic growth engines through operational excellence.

To reiterate, all significant value is created through innovation, generation, operation, and transaction. It is the cross-boundary, systemic optimization of one or more of these bundles of activity with respect to the drivers of cost, speed, quality, waste, working capital, productivity, and output that drives enterprise results. Thus, good strategy will always focus on one or more of these bundles and the value they generate. **See Diagram 4.**

Chapter 2 - Strategy and Capability

VALUE CREATION

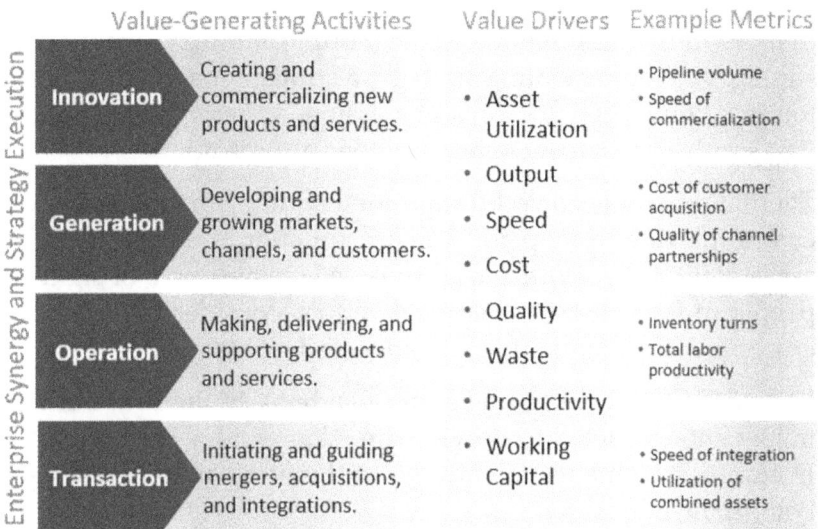

Diagram 4

Strategy is about making good choices with less than perfect information and utilizing limited resources to serve customers in superior ways. Becoming a more strategic leader involves first understanding the nature of strategy and capability, and second, the use of a disciplined process for exploring strategic questions at the right altitude: on a daily basis in small informal ways *and* in formal strategic planning settings. A strategic mindset is both analytical and creative, short- and long-term, internal and external, and narrow and broad in nature.

With respect to the external environment *and* internal organization, leaders can engage others in collaborative SWOT-type exercises, identifying strengths, weaknesses, opportunities, and threats. This analysis should include an examination of the trends affecting the enterprise and the ecosystem in which it operates, represented by the acronym PEST: political, economic, social, and technological forces. From this foundation, strategic goals, imperatives, and initiatives can be developed into a strategic roadmap, or put more simply, the strategy map.

Developing the Strategy Map

One of the most helpful frameworks for a leader is the strategy map. Whether the leader is developing strategy, influencing strategy, or implementing strategy, a strategy map is very useful tool for connecting the dots of mission, values, goals, capabilities, results, and other elements of the value chain.

There is no single correct design for a strategy map. Leaders can create a strategy map for a team, function, business unit, or entire enterprise. With the purpose of creating line-of-sight for people to focus their collaborative effort, consider the following example from a marketing and advertising firm.

Imagine one-page with the entire playbook of the firm outlined in just enough detail to provide direction and focus activity. **See Diagram 5.** Elements and *excerpts* of the firm's map from top-to-bottom included:

- **Mission:** Market leader in marketing services for the retail and hospitality industry. Provide social media platform and client service that is best in the industry.

- **Strategic goals**: Grow revenue through new business unit that focuses on helping on-line retailers build bricks-and-mortar outlets. Improve operational efficiencies in call center services to manage workload and increase sales for clients.

- **Scorecard metrics**: Employee engagement; client satisfaction; new client acquisition; call center productivity; total margin management; revenue growth; and cash flow and ebitda.

- **Strategic imperatives**: Find new sources of revenue and grow ideal client base. Increase call center utilization. Increase client utilization of marketing platform. Preserve pricing and increase margins in core services.

- **Strategic capabilities**: New market development; client relationship management; marketing platform innovation; call center management.

- **Core capabilities**: New client on-boarding, client engagement management; talent and performance management; cash flow management.

- **Business priorities**: Specific priorities that directly relate to the strategic goals and imperatives of the enterprise, and that get reviewed and updated quarterly to ensure needed attention, resourcing, and progress.
- **Values and culture**: Action orientation of agility, initiative, diligence, accountability, and reliability. Great work environment with the attributes of professional, positive, learning, growing, and rewarding.

STRATEGY MAP EXCERPT

Mission

Leader in demand creation services fore the retail and hospitality industry. Provide marketing and service platform that is best-in-class.

Strategic Goals

Grow revenue through new business unit market penetration. Improve operational efficiencies to manage workload and drive sales.

Scorecard Metrics

Employee Engagement	Client Satisfaction	New Client Acquisition	Productivity and Margins	Profitable Growth

Strategic Imperatives

New sources of revenue	Call center utilization	Marketing platform use	Pricing preservation	Margin preservation

Capabilities

Market development	Client management	Performance management	Call center management	Financial optimization

Business priorities

[3-5 business priorities that relate to strategic goals and imperatives] Example: Engage 3 new clients to develop new store strategy.

Culture and values

Action orientation: agility, accountability, and reliability. Positive environment: learning, performing, growing, rewarding.

Diagram 5

While the strategy map for the firm is an annual exercise, business priorities that guide daily work activity are updated quarterly. While strategic goals and imperatives have a year-long lifespan, leaders understand the firm needs 3-4 key priorities to rally around that are aligned with the strategy map *and* focused on immediate needs of a constantly changing environment.

Strategy is all about setting direction and it is *both* static and dynamic. Every enterprise needs both anchoring goals and evolving priorities. The aspiring leader learns how to be strategic at varying altitudes as needed to guide this activity.

Building the Customer and Capability Flywheel

Professional service firms often struggle to leverage client impact in driving profitable growth. In the crowded and frenetic services space it can be very hard to maintain a distinctive value proposition and build an enduring brand. A key differentiator is a firm's ability to demonstrate value and show impact in ways that resonate with clients and align with their evolving needs.

Consider the small to mid-sized firm on a growth trajectory. It has several clients that dominate its portfolio, a few proven rainmakers, a mix of recurring and non-recurring revenue streams, and a group of busy, talented consultants. The firm is challenged with standing-out in the marketplace, finding new clients to expand its portfolio, prioritizing investments for growth, focusing on distinctive offerings, and smoothing the lumpiness in revenue and cash flow. How might client impact assessment help address these challenges?

Each firm converts its value proposition into value creation through core capabilities. This is the customer-capability flywheel. While most firms rightfully emphasize service excellence as the key to success, they often lack a rigorous method for assessing client impact. Thus, there are related soft-spots in capabilities that serve to limit profitable growth. Capabilities that are often affected include business development, service innovation, service delivery, client management, and talent management.

In this context, what are the common challenges in building the customer-capability flywheel? And how do these translate into leadership challenges and needs?

Here are specific solutions for each of the five core capabilities and their link to client value and impact.

Business development. A key challenge is the lack of clarity and focus of the firm's value proposition. Flywheel firms are specialized in service offerings that focus on specific verticals. They have a deep understanding of industry trends and forces, and pervasive client pain points, and use these insights to tell a compelling story about the impact of their work on client business results. At the same time, they do not limit themselves to serving only certain industries.

Service innovation. A key challenge is disorganized product and service innovation. Flywheel firms balance opportunistic project-driven innovation with strategic new offerings that build on current services. With a deep understanding of clients and industries, and a clear mission and value proposition, they develop new services that meet specific underserved or emerging needs. They leverage but don't over-rely on trendy technologies and bandwagon programs.

Service delivery. A key challenge is the lack of synergy across consulting practices and client project teams. Flywheel firms are very intentional about creating cross-practice and cross-client collaboration. Drawing from client impact insights, they syndicate proven frameworks, tools, and approaches to make each practice better in serving clients and developing new business. And they use feedback loops to inform client prospecting, proposals, and project work in real-time.

Client management. A key challenge is inconsistency in client engagement, relationship-building, and impact assessment. Flywheel firms use client feedback to ensure every interaction contributes to the client experience. They are purposeful in how they on-board the client, communicate with the client team, manage the work, discuss progress, and assess impact. And they preserve the premium pricing of their services.

Talent management. A key challenge is a lack of business acumen in having strategic client conversations. Flywheel firms develop competencies for robust situational discussions about the client's business model, operating model, and value chains.

Their people are better able to help clients establish a clear line of sight between the need, the work, and business results. In doing so, they also uncover opportunities that lead to new top-priority, high-margin projects.

Faced with the need to become integrated in serving clients and going to market, consider the consulting firm that implemented a more rigorous process for assessing client impact beyond perceptions of value. Inculcating the process helped inform key firm initiatives of target client acquisition, client relationship management, cross-practice collaboration, and consultant skill-building. As a result, the firm realized highly profitable growth in a very competitive marketplace.

High-performing professional service firms pay attention to the client value and firm capability flywheel. They know the flywheel is critical to driving future growth through delivering measurable impact, building client relationships, and acquiring new clients. Leaders and their firms are well-served to develop this virtuous cycle.

Leading with an Entrepreneurial Spirit

Entrepreneurship is the process by which ideas are generated, developed, and implemented to create value. Intrapreneurs create new value-creation entities in an existing organization while entrepreneurs create new entities in the external marketplace. Both require an entrepreneurial spirit for success.

Very similar to a strategic mindset, an entrepreneurial spirit and mindset is characterized by deep curiosity about the world and commitment to learning; ability to recognize patterns and integrate ideas to create new solutions; bias for action, experimentation, and execution; comfortableness with uncertainty and ambiguity; ability to shed limiting beliefs and not take failure personally; and desire to build something valuable that endures.

While it is true that often founders of companies are unable to make the long-term transition into management and leadership, the effective leader-entrepreneur is both possible and needed. There are several strategic practices for leaders who are already on an entrepreneurial path or considering this direction:

Chapter 2 - Strategy and Capability

- Stay current on trends, patterns, and resource flows within an industry and its broader ecosystem.
- Explore and understand pain points and unmet needs of potential customers, channels, and markets.
- Develop value creation ideas but even more important develop quality relationships within the ecosystem.
- Initiate new projects to explore ideas and develop specialized expertise through new experiences.
- Pursue new business concepts from the perspectives of the customer, the investor, and the owner.

Many young professionals are leaders of their own business in the gig economy. But do they—do you?—view yourself as an entrepreneur and leader of a business, or merely as a contractor?

Consider the aspiring leader-solopreneur who developed the following plan for building a consulting practice in the underserved marketplace of construction project management:

- Continue learning and developing specialized knowledge in large-scale infrastructure construction projects.
- Further develop the strategic storyline of pain points and needs in large-scale contracting and project management.
- Develop relationships within regional associations, planning commissions, and construction enterprises.
- Offer a free, up-front diagnostic to potential buyers to educate them on efficiency opportunities and collect data.
- Master leading-edge project management technologies for the construction space and offer insights into their usage.
- Develop a mission and value proposition outlining impact from the construction leader and contractor perspectives.

Several themes are noteworthy here: specializing in a growth industry; building relationships with buyers of services; understanding the flows of money and other resources; and, attaching early to the coattails of trending practices and technologies.

Formally starting a new venture—solo or with a partner—begins with exploring these questions (similar to strategic questions):

- What is our mission? What business are we in? What problem are we solving? Why will we solve it better?
- Who will we serve? Who will pay us and for what? What services or products will we provide?
- How will we make money? What are our financial expectations? How and when will we get paid?
- What will we be the best at? What will we be really good at? How will we succeed?
- How will we get one customer or client? How will we get 3-4 more clients after that? How will we focus our outreach?
- What investment is required, for what, and from whom? What is our critical path forward for the next few months?

Dispelling a few common myths, the entrepreneurial leader does not have to keep ideas a total secret, move fast, and be under the radar; does not have to be an amazing visionary; and, does not have to be a great networker or fundraiser.

The aspiring leader can pursue a calling with a commitment to integrity and ethics, stable and healthy life habits, and a purpose and passion that may or may not always involve a paycheck. Patience, diligence, and resilience will pay-off in the long-run.

Linking Strategy Execution and Transformation

In some circles today, strategy and strategic planning are unwisely considered old-school concepts. Arguments are made along the lines of "the world is changing too fast to spend time on strategy that is quickly obsolete." But strategy is essential: new lean and agile approaches to business will undoubtedly fail if they are rudderless. The real imperative is to change the emphasis of strategy from planning to execution. Organizations must adapt and co-evolve with their environments through focused and integrated strategies. This strategic co-evolution is the new transformation where change is truly constant.

Pursuing transformation as a discrete initiative rather than as fundamental to the continuous evolution of the enterprise is a primary reason so many change efforts fail or underperform.

In the outmoded "unfreeze-change-refreeze" model, change is viewed as a "thing" that is made to stick. In organizations that transform—that is, effectively *evolve*—ongoing change is built into the strategic roadmap and cultural fabric as a matter of doing business. Transformation is not implementing new initiatives; rather, it is about guiding how the organization continuously improves the way it operates and creates value.

It is true that over the course of an organization's lifecycle, there are *critical-state* inflections that require breakthrough change or renewal, such as when early stage companies cross the chasm from proof-of-concept to building scale, or when mature companies reinvent their business model due to permanent marketplace disruptions. As the critical situations become more frequent, leaders can approach change as the expected and natural evolution of the enterprise.

When change is framed as a discrete initiative, efforts fail for historically persistent reasons. The reasons are consistent with the general causes of poor enterprise performance outlined in expectancy theory. They include a lack of leadership alignment and management commitment; a lack of a clear business case and roadmap; a lack of clear goals and priorities; a lack of employee engagement; a lack of needed capability, tools, and resources; and a lack of results-driven feedback and rewards.

The inverse of these common causes of failure is the blueprint for success. Transformation requires an understanding of what is changing, why it is changing, why it is important, what is expected of people, what is in it for them, and what success looks like. People will support and participate in change if it makes sense to them; they know what to do; they see others doing it; they are enabled to do it; and they get rewarded for it. And people will support change with high levels of commitment when they have played a role in deciding and shaping the change itself.

The approach to effective transformation is therefore no different than the approach to strategy execution. It guides what and how work gets done and by whom. In exploring the progress and impact of transformation, the leader can examine seven key areas of opportunity.

Business understanding: There is a well-defined and broadly-understood case for change that requires greater business literacy across the organization. There is an acknowledgment of the everyday reality of competing priorities, funding limitations, and resource constraints, and how this challenging terrain can be kept in perspective and navigated. People deep in the organization and on the front lines understand the dynamic nature of the economic model: how customers are acquired, how cash is generated, and how money is made — and how these fundamentals are changing.

Strategy mapping: The roadmap for change is a part, or an extension, of the enterprise strategy. It shows why and how the business model and strategy will evolve to better acquire and serve customers, make money and create value, and survive and thrive in a dynamic marketplace, while preserving core values and strengths. Specific milestones are established to reinforce the desired urgency, cadence, and speed required of the change. In this way, gaining and sustaining traction with transformation is no different than with strategy execution.

Role-modeling: There is strong leadership alignment and commitment that is demonstrated through the role-modeling of new mindsets and behaviors. People across the organization see leaders and managers behaving differently, consistent with new requirements of the business. These are demonstrated in a disciplined manner in how priorities are managed, resources are allocated, meetings are run, decisions are made, information is shared, and collaboration is facilitated.

Performance reporting: The performance scorecard and reporting system is evolving based on the changing needs of the enterprise. New forward-looking execution metrics, such as working capital, brand reputation, and time with new customers, are balanced with standard backward-looking financial metrics, such as margin growth, operating profit, and return on invested capital. New metrics provide helpful information in real-time. Outcome-based milestones remain critical here as transformation activity evolves.

Active mobilizing: There are a variety of guided efforts underway to engage people at all levels, in small and large forums, and through "high-touch" and "high-tech" methods to execute the transformation roadmap. People are directly involved in reengineering key processes and changing how work gets done in teams. They are actively engaged in creating needed congruence between the strategic change that is required and the work activities they are responsible for on a daily basis.

Muscle-building: There is focused learning at the enterprise, group, and individual levels. Strategic and core enterprise capabilities that create competitive advantage, such as demand creation through customer intimacy, are well-translated into group abilities and individual competencies, such as great customer service, that are then reinforced through both formal and informal training, development, and feedback processes.

Performance reinforcing: The performance and reward systems are evolving to reinforce desired mindsets, behaviors, and results. Financial reward programs support the changes people are being asked to make in carrying out *both* old and new responsibilities in parallel. These systems directly reinforce the achievement of key priorities and outcomes at the individual, group, and enterprise levels. Incentives focus on *both* operational drivers and financial results.

Based on the seven areas described above, enterprise leaders can assess and improve the current state of transformation—and thus strategy execution—by exploring ten diagnostic questions:

- Is the business strategy integrated with the transformation roadmap, where the *what, why,* and *how* of change are given equal emphasis?
- Are leaders visibly and consistently role-modeling new mindsets and behaviors in their daily meetings and interactions—are new habits replacing old ones?

- Are people applying new capabilities and competencies directly related to the evolving business model?
- Are program and project managers achieving milestone-based and customer-driven objectives that create value?
- Are people focused on doing work that directly relates to the value creation bundles and value drivers such as output, quality, cost, quality, and productivity?
- Do performance reports show the milestone-based migration to new metrics that reflect the evolving business model?
- Do everyday conversations openly address old-world vs. new-world market dynamics, competing priorities, and resource challenges?
- Are customers and partners actively engaged in helping develop and improve new ways of doing business?
- Is change-related information shared broadly and deeply in the organization, and in useful ways that can be applied on-the-job in real-time?
- Are leaders accountable and rewarded for demonstrating behaviors and achieving results critical to the transformation?

In closing, the characteristics of effective change overlap nicely with those of effective day-to-day strategy execution, reflecting the timeless qualities of clarity, focus, agility, and discipline. Transformation is not separate from daily operations; it is integral to them.

CHAPTER 3

Work, Networks, and Productivity

Leading companies are much more productive with higher operating margins and faster growth than other firms.
It is easy to see that leaders risk ignoring productivity at their own peril.

Introduction

This chapter explores the fundamentals of defining, improving, and measuring value creation with an emphasis on productivity and productive collaboration within groups and networks. The chapter emphasizes the importance of and challenges involved with improving the productivity of knowledge workers.

As you read and think about this chapter, consider how your impact as a leader is linked to your effectiveness in engaging people to collaborate productively across organizational boundaries. Consider how new definitions of productivity and value are needed in our digital and networked world.

In exploring this chapter, consider a few questions: What aspects of productivity and value creation will you strengthen or begin developing to grow as a leader? What new mindsets, behaviors, practices, and abilities are needed? What topics would you like to study further to deepen your understanding?

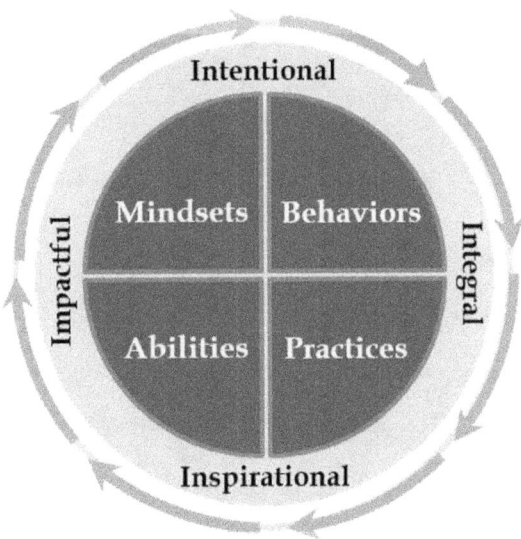

Diagram 1

Every day we are bombarded with productivity "hacks" to do more as individuals. These self-help tips entirely miss the point because they get the unit of measurement wrong.

Whether you only lead yourself, or lead others too, true productivity is measured by group outputs that create real value and that are often *not* driven by the efficiency of individual activities.

Chapter 3 - Work, Networks, and Productivity

Awakening to the Productivity Crisis

In the digital age and ecosystem economy, leaders are not paying enough attention to operations and the true drivers of value. As they pursue complex frontiers of networked operating models, enterprise agility initiatives, and cognitive technology platforms, leadership teams are poised to make the same mistakes they have made in the past about enterprise productivity and its impact on sustained profitability and value creation.

It has been called a problem, a puzzle, and a paradox. Productivity *growth* is at very low levels in many organizations. While there has been some recent good news, the gap between the most productive firms and everyone else is still increasing. In a recent study, Bain found that leading companies are 40% more productive with 30-50% higher operating margins and faster growth. It is easy to see that leaders risk ignoring productivity at their own peril.

Total productivity reflects how well the enterprise invests, allocates, and utilizes resources to perform value-generating activity. It reflects the optimization of cost, quality, waste, and efficiency. It is a primary driver of operating margin, economic profit, and real wages. With the future of work already here, leaders are focusing on agility and speed, but are leaving out a serious exploration of two prevalent organizational realities.

First, individual efficiencies have not translated into total productivity growth in most organizations. People are doing more work faster, but they spend too much time on low-value activities that contribute little to profitable growth. While they are seemingly more efficient in handling increasing workloads, their work is too fragmented and frenetic, with high switching costs and much wasted effort. As the management guru Peter Drucker once said, "There is surely nothing quite so useless as doing with great efficiency what should not be done at all."

Consider the consumer products company that studied middle management and found very little overlap between the most important value-adding work and what people spent most of their time on each day. As a result, the firm implemented bold new rules of work design that reduced unproductive time sinks and refocused activity on critical customer needs.

Second, digital technologies also have not translated into total productivity growth in most organizations. People have much greater access to data and are more connected, but spend too much time sitting in meetings, using instant communications, figuring out complicated systems, and doing unnecessary analytics. While people are doing more work in teams, groups, and networks, the quality of conversations is going down. To paraphrase the renowned economist Robert Solow, "The digital age can be seen everywhere except in the productivity data."

Consider the life sciences company that resisted the allure of a new sales and operations planning technology, and instead, replaced redundant functional meetings with fewer, more collaborative, cross-functional working sessions. As a result, the firm successfully implemented a new supply chain strategy and realized substantial increases in operating margin without buying any expensive shiny new objects.

In a recent study, most companies are redesigning their organizations to be more dynamic, team-centric, and connected. But what about becoming more productive? With this question in mind, leaders should consider pursuing five imperatives:

- **Change mindset from "do more with less" to "do less to achieve more."** Create space for open conversations throughout the organization about the new business realities and the natural tensions involving agility, speed, *and* productivity. Engage people in dialog about the need to think and work differently, the wisdom of slowing down to speed up, and the competing forces involved with creativity, flexibility, *and* execution. A good first step is to develop a compelling narrative about the drivers of systemic productivity and the implications for enterprise synergy and collaboration.

- **Renew the focus on core value-driving activities.** Apply more rigor to fully evaluating the disruptive impact on productivity before restructuring businesses, investing in enterprise technologies, or adopting big data platforms. Rebalance emphasis from top-down planning for functions to top-down guidance for cross-functional value networks. Refocus energy and resources on the core capabilities of innovation, commercialization, customer acquisition, and supply chain (operations). A good first step is to develop new definitions, metrics, and baselines of systemic productivity for these four value creating bundles.

- **Create the conditions for more productive collaboration.** Develop new communication channels within networks of activity that foster high quality conversations. Break down structural silos, hierarchical controls, and decision protocols that waste effort and block natural synergies from emerging. Utilize new tools and technologies *only if* they facilitate collaborative *and* productive work activity. A good first step is to implement a new process for supporting and synchronizing teams that emphasizes a critical few strategic goals and value-drivers.

- **Establish new norms of meeting and communicating:** Role-model new ways of working that reduce unnecessary busyness and work fragmentation. Reduce the number of meetings and total meeting time by 25-33 percent. Reduce the standard time in regular meetings from one-hour to 25 or 45 minutes. Implement usage protocols to reduce the time spent on emails and other transactional messaging. A good first step is to implement a simple and disciplined methodology to conduct agenda-based and outcome-oriented meetings where real work gets done.

- **Accelerate development of new leadership capabilities.** Identify pivotal leaders and leadership teams throughout the organization that guide value-generating work. Integrate talent development and performance management programs to better reinforce the optimization of agility, speed, and productivity. Accelerate development through action-learning cohorts that work on enterprise productivity improvement projects. A good first step is to engage distributed leaders in workshops to co-create new behaviors that foster more organic and productive interactions.

Consider the financial services company that is growing both organically and through acquisition. To manage disruption during this transformative period, the firm emphasizes total productivity when exploring technologies, improving processes, developing leaders, and managing performance. Leaders engage groups of people in conversations about the relationship between values, culture, productivity, and profit. As a result, the firm consistently meets aggressive revenue and profit goals.

In high-performing firms, leaders pay attention to productivity. They inspire people throughout the enterprise to drive real productivity improvement. They focus less on local efficiencies and more on systemic productivity gains. And they accelerate development of new mindsets, behaviors, and practices across the organization that help create the conditions for a more collaborative and productive culture.

Defining Productivity and Value Creation

Organizations today operate in a complex, dynamic, and networked global business environment. They are challenged with rapidly evolving business models and customer acquisition channels; decentralized supply chains and partner-based ecosystems; patchwork systems of legacy and emerging information technologies; rise of big analytics and fragmentation of knowledge work; unproven modes of digital communication and collaboration; and strong marketplace incentives for accelerated revenue and profit gains. In this whirlwind reality, organizations are more confused than ever about how to sustain value creation.

Firms continue to spend vast amounts of resources on strategies and technologies to lower costs and increase efficiencies. But they often are unable to answer the most basic question of whether productivity, and thus value creation, has actually improved as a result. For example, while very unpopular to suggest, it is not at all clear whether highly expensive enterprise resource planning systems have driven productivity gains that reflect expected returns on investment. Even more fundamental, while most organizations have relatively sophisticated approaches to financial measurement, they do not have good definitions or metrics for productivity growth and its link to financial outcomes.

The definition of productivity and the metrics used to support it can vary by business model, nature of work performed, and employee segment. Just as there is no single way to define productivity, there is no single way to measure it either. In the broadest sense, productivity reflects how well a system uses its resources—financial, human, technological, and natural—to transform inputs into outputs and create value. In the narrowest sense, it can be defined simply as output produced per hours worked or as value created per dollar spent.

A new leadership mindset and management approach is needed to address the enterprise productivity challenge. A closer examination of the work activities and interactions that create value requires greater visibility within the organization to understand and isolate key productivity drivers. In getting serious about the current state of productivity, organization leaders can consider the following questions:

- How does the organization currently define and measure productivity? How does it link it to value creation?
- What are the organization's beliefs, hypotheses, and facts regarding its current productivity levels?
- To what extent are productivity metrics used in managing and improving the performance of the enterprise?
- What are the drivers of productivity improvement today and how will these drivers evolve going forward?
- How are investments in people, such as compensation, job design, and training linked to productivity improvement?

Regardless of what an enterprise produces—a service, a product, a piece of information, a unit of wealth, or a psychological experience—its productivity in doing so ultimately determines the degree to which it can create value over the long term. Enterprise productivity is not the simple sum of the productivity of individuals or groups. It is highly dependent on how effectively people interact in loosely-defined networks, access and exchange information using a variety of sources, and solve problems and make decisions within fluid situations. This is especially true of knowledge workers, where work often involves competing priorities, shifting contexts, and fragmented activities. Therefore, developing a culture of productivity requires a shared definition of productivity, a more sophisticated understanding of the drivers of productivity, and the right mix of investments in those drivers over a sustained period of time.

Again, productivity is how well a system uses its resources to achieve its goals. Productivity is not the same thing as performance. It is more objective, and almost always determined relative to quantitative inputs and investments, whereas performance is more subjective and often defined relative to qualitative expectations and goals. Productivity is also not the same thing as engagement. Productivity reflects the actual conversion of inputs into outputs, while engagement reflects more of an intent, commitment, and effort to do so.

Productivity is not the same thing as personal efficiency. Every day we are bombarded with productivity "hacks" to do more as individuals. These self-help tips entirely miss the point because they get the unit of measurement wrong. Whether you only lead yourself, or lead others too, true productivity is measured by group outputs that create real value and that are often *not* driven by the efficiency of individual activities.

These are the main causes of unproductive strategy execution that "crowd-out" value-creating activity:

- Annual planning and budgeting processes that voraciously consume time, frustrate people, and poorly allocate resources.
- Shifting and competing priorities that create confusion, cause miscommunication and impede coordination across functions.
- Onerous analytics and unintegrated databases that paralyze the organization's ability to make decisions and obstruct action at the speed of business.
- Too many meetings and too much instant communication that distract people and contribute to the extreme fragmentation and switching costs of their work.
- Reorganization and restructuring that hinder the ability to gain traction and build momentum for driving priorities.

- Work processes and decision-making protocols that are insufficient or out of balance: either too detailed and controlling or too general and flexible.

- Overuse of consultants who peddle trendy programs and new technologies that are too expensive, highly disruptive, and non-systemic in nature.

- Too many, too few, or the wrong indicators, metrics, and incentives for reinforcing the most critical activities and outcomes for creating value.

With these productivity-killers in mind, there are proven and timeless characteristics of highly productive organizations. The leadership teams in these firms:

- Unify their workforce around a simple, elevating, and customer-centric mission and strategy that are clearly tied to the fundamentals of their business model and sources of competitive advantage.

- Build a productivity flywheel over time, avoid the program du jour, and take an integrated approach to improving the effectiveness of cross-functional business processes and value networks.

- Execute strategies with discipline, realism, and follow-through. They hold people accountable, measure progress, and stay objective and open about the performance of the business and the need for improvement.

- Create just enough structure, minimize bureaucracy, continuously break down silos, wisely allocate resources, and have a very low tolerance for wasted effort of any kind.

- Are less concerned about doing more work faster and more concerned about doing the right work better. They eliminate low-value work and minimize multitasking and fragmented work activity that carry high switching costs.

- Embrace lean systems with very high standards for quality, ruthlessly eliminate all forms of waste, emphasize lead over lag metrics, and use rigorous continuous improvement methods that start with the customer perspective.

- Foster high quality interactions between people, facilitate effective group collaboration, and minimize meetings, which, when used, are agenda-based where real work gets done.
- Treat performance management and development as a key business process. They use metric-driven information to openly discuss performance gaps and prioritize improvement opportunities.

Consider the university hospital that increased the productivity of its operating rooms. Leaders chartered a cross-functional perioperative services team to complete an extensive analysis. They found the potential for millions of dollars in revenue and cost savings from low room utilization and surgery throughput.

The team implemented new processes for improving operating room operations and total productivity. Consistent with several practices outlined above, the team focused on higher quality a) schedules to manage start-times and caseflow, b) standards to reduce rework in room turns, c) conversations to reduce team miscommunication, and d) resources to provide faster real-time systems support. Leaders focused on the key relationship between quality — doing it right the first time — and total productivity.

Exploring the Senior Leadership Perspective

While firms continue to spend vast amounts of resources to lower costs and increase efficiencies, they often are unable to answer the most basic question of whether productivity and real value have actually improved as a result. In this context, important questions arise about the degree to which enterprise leaders care about productivity, how they think about it, and what their organizations are doing to improve it.

This section summarizes the perspective of twenty senior leaders from a variety of industries: industrial and consumer products, healthcare, agriculture, transportation, and financial and professional services. All have been or are currently in CEO, COO, or CFO roles. And all offered compelling and often consistent views on the importance of productivity, the evolving nature of work, and the risks associated with not paying enough attention to operations in the current business landscape.

In summarizing these conversations, a compelling storyline emerged. The main narrative is captured as follows:

- Total productivity is vitally important but not given enough attention at the enterprise level. It is a primary driver of operating margin and economic profit.
- A more strategic approach is needed to drive productivity improvement of innovation, customer acquisition, and making and delivering products and services.
- A shift is needed to move the pendulum back from financial engineering to basic operational effectiveness and disciplined execution that ruthlessly eliminates all forms of redundancy, excess capacity, and waste.
- Incentives in the marketplace, especially in public companies, do not reinforce or reward for productivity-driven value creation; instead, they reward for fast top-line growth from financial manipulation and mergers and acquisitions.
- People in organizations are *not* working on the right things. They spend most of their time doing low-value added activity involving meetings, emails, messaging, and analytics, resulting in analysis paralysis and slow decision-making.
- Other widespread barriers to enterprise productivity include constant and disruptive leadership discontinuity, integration chaos from M&A activity, persistent functional silos, and burdensome technologies.
- The drivers of productivity improvement include strategic clarity, prioritized focus, organizational alignment, less fragmented work, systemic thinking, and lean-agile skillsets.
- Leadership and management must pay more attention to ongoing performance management as a key business process for driving value creation.

Seven detailed themes emerged from these conversations, consistent with the storyline captured above, and summarized below along with supporting quotes.

1. Better understand and define productivity.

Productivity means different things in different organizations for different business models. Traditionally, productivity has been equated with labor productivity and considered a driver of profit margins. In some industries over the years, productivity has been stigmatized due to its perceived equivalence to across-the-board cost-cutting and headcount reduction. It might even be considered an outdated term or concept. But productivity is much more than that: it is how well an organization use its resources to create real value.

There is no question that total productivity is critical to the success of an enterprise, but it often does not get enough attention, or it is hidden in operational and financial metrics. There is a basic inability in most organizations to directly measure overall productivity, and because of this, little attention is paid specifically to the drivers of and barriers to productivity improvement. This has been magnified by the shift in many organizations away from healthy operational effectiveness to the sugar-high of financial engineering results.

In their own words: *I'm not sure how productive we are, that's a great question. Productivity is really important, but we don't use the term very much, or talk about it directly. Productivity is just hard to measure outside of core operations. There's a stigma about productivity going back many years to the days of downsizing. Productivity is the power that drives the long-term sustainability of the company.*

2. Start with strategy to improve productivity.

There is a need to broaden the concept of productivity from labor to the enterprise. Enterprise productivity requires a strategic approach to running the business day-to-day, co-evolving with the marketplace, and preparing for the future. This involves the systemic alignment of activities that grow revenue and generate profit to create value.

Specifically, the enterprise must improve the productivity of the four value generators of sustained results: innovation, commercialization, customer acquisition, and the production and delivery of products and services. Principles of productive operations should be applied across key functions, processes, and networks. Much

Chapter 3 - Work, Networks, and Productivity

more attention is needed—beginning with a strategic map that provides clarity, direction, and alignment—to how the organization operates and executes in a disciplined manner.

In their own words: *Productivity is all about day-to-day execution, but requires thoughtful strategy. Enterprise productivity is what drives sustainable, profitable growth. Alignment is the most important thing to productivity. The value chain begins with productivity, which drives margin improvement, profit, and value creation. Strategic direction is needed to build a culture of productivity.*

3. Shift from a financial to operational mindset.

In public companies today, and in many private ones too, there is too much emphasis on M&A-driven revenue growth and financially manipulated earnings, and too little emphasis on operations that drive real economic profit. Capital investment is too low, investment horizons are too short, and investment hurdles are too high. CEOs with short life-expectancies and even shorter attention spans are incented to drive top-line metrics while engineering short-term profit.

In addition to constant and disruptive mergers and acquisitions, organizations remain mired in annual budgeting and capital planning processes that focus on expenditures, zero-budget growth, and cost-of-capital analytics that take up a lot of time and deliver little value.

A much more balanced approach is needed, with leadership courage as the starting point. Regardless of external forces, the pendulum needs to move back toward building stronger, healthier, more productive, and sustainable businesses that create real value. The lifespans of organizations are not shortening because of the "new reality" of the marketplace; they are shortening because we are incenting the wrong things and leaders are too accepting of this dynamic.

In their own words: *We must maximize productivity in all areas of the business to drive profitable growth. There is a lack of courage, patience, and long-term thinking among senior executives. It seems like we spend more time talking about capital planning than we spend on actually making investments to drive productivity and profitability. The market rewards for revenue more than profitability. Senior leaders* are fixated on short-term revenue and profit bumps that reward themselves and shareholders. Keeping revenue and profit growth in balance is the key to value creation.

4. Focus on things that matter and stop doing things that don't.

Improving enterprise value creation requires a dramatic increase in focus on key priorities and work activities that truly matter. Today we are able to do more work faster, but we often spend too much time on the wrong things. We have too many toys and technologies, too many metrics and analytics, and too much data. We spend too much time in too many meetings and confuse doing emails and Slack-chats with getting real work done. We still work in silos and struggle to communicate, coordinate, and collaborate in productive ways.

While people and functions often seem to be more efficient, their work activities do not necessarily translate into—*and can actually detract from*—systemic enterprise productivity improvement and value creation. ERP systems are neutral *at best*, unless they are implemented intelligently to drive total productivity instead of functional or process efficiency. For all of the talk about efficiency, there are still high levels of redundancy and waste.

People spend the majority of their time doing low-priority, non-value-added activity. They need to stop doing a lot of it. Big data and big analytics are often big distractions. Much more of the work people do both individually and in teams should directly contribute to the three most critical value drivers that span across functions and processes: finding and keeping customers, creating new products and services, and making and delivering those products and services.

In their own words: *Business is not any more rapid or complex than it used to be — we are just able to do more analysis with more data more quickly. In lean studies, less than five-percent of the work people do is value-adding and this is true of our organization. Radical change is needed to get people to work differently. The misalignment of priorities is a productivity killer. When everything is a priority, nothing is a priority. If you add a new program or project, eliminate two others. Technology is never designed to improve productivity — it is designed for control.*

5. Feed the hedgehog rather than whack a mole.

Enterprise productivity requires greater leadership continuity and management attention. Operationally excellent firms emphasize very high levels of quality and very low levels of waste, while managing cost and realizing productivity gains. Instead of applying the hedge-hog approach where management attention is on the flywheel of fundamentals, leaders today deploy strategies more akin to "whack-a-mole" that are often disruptive, non-systemic, and unsustainable.

Instead of focusing on the alignment, synergy, and productivity of business processes and value networks, organizations continue to focus on restructuring and installing trendy new technologies to drive results. But the barriers to real productivity gains are often not fixed, and are even magnified: people still operate in silos, processes and systems are not well-integrated, and there is a revolving door of talent in key roles.

In their own words: *Enterprise productivity requires keeping the business model simple. We want to pursue the slower flywheel than create fast-motion chaos. Big technologies can bury the organization in inefficiencies. Leadership discontinuity is a huge problem. With restructuring and mergers, we are in an integration haze. We move the dial on results with new initiatives, but then shift focus, and don't sustain the change or hardwire it into the organization. Process improvement is critical to productivity which is critical to profitability.*

6. Develop new skills deep within the workforce.

The root cause of low productivity is spending too much time doing the wrong things, albeit more efficiently but in non-systemic ways. Across industries—and even in traditional manufacturing organizations—knowledge work at all levels of the enterprise is plagued by high levels of wasted activity and low levels of real productivity.

New skills and competencies are needed for professionals, managers, and leaders to better navigate rapidly evolving business models and more fragmented marketplaces. To achieve more productive, value-adding outcomes, knowledge workers need greater capability in the following areas: discerning needed analytics, collaborating in teams across boundaries, focusing on a critical few priorities, fluidly adapting to change, and applying lean and agile principles to work practices and processes.

In their own words: *The skills of people must evolve if they are to remain productive. We need more competence in basic operations, not in finance or marketing. The secret sauce of our success is groups of people improving their own work processes. We are using lean principles and six-sigma across the organization to drive margin improvement. People need to be more discerning about prioritizing work and collecting and analyzing information. People need new skills to create a culture of productivity and value creation.*

7. Manage performance more effectively.

More attention is needed to effectively manage and improve performance. Most companies are continually disappointed in their performance management program since they treat it as a program and not as a business process. Organizations struggle with performance ratings, feedback conversations, and the linkages to pay, and then often fail in trying to fix these problems through automation.

A new approach is needed. Good performance management starts at the strategic, enterprise level with clear priorities and value creation map. It starts with leaders. It requires an understanding of the evolving business model. It emphasizes coaching and development. And it replaces personal efficiency and goal achievement with group-based productivity and key results.

In their own words: *We want people to be doing only what they are supposed to be doing. We strive for role clarity and focused attention on what is most important. Knowledge workers need a guiding light to help them deal with the fragmentation of their work. We need to change the emphasis from backward-looking assessment to forward looking development. We need new productivity metrics for the future.*

From the perspectives of these leaders, the case for rethinking enterprise productivity is clear. The nature of these conversations, focused on the topic of productivity, revealed the challenges organizations face each day to create value, and the desire to return to the fundamentals of good business practice. A new leadership mindset and strategic approach is needed to refocus on what really matters, emphasizing enterprise productivity as a key to healthy, profitable, and sustained growth.

Improving the Effectiveness of Knowledge Work

Organizations and their leaders spend too much time and energy trying to "engage" people in their work and not enough on helping them be more productive together, especially when it comes to knowledge workers. This is one of the main reasons why so many enterprises suffer from low productivity growth, affecting overall output, competitiveness, and wages.

Work is defined as coordinated activity that is carried out to perform the functions of the organization. Knowledge work is typically non-routine, information-driven, highly cognitive, and very collaborative. It often involves a high degree of interaction and coordination, shifting and competing priorities, and ambiguity and uncertainty. Much of the work takes place in meetings, on project teams, and within a variety of groups and networks. The work itself is often fragmented, discontinuous, and loosely defined. The productivity challenge of knowledge workers — including both managers and professionals — is only increasing with the realities of doing business with the volatility, distraction, and velocity of today's environment.

While technology has undoubtedly enabled people to do more work faster, this has not translated into system-wide enterprise productivity. Consider the case of a technology company that found about fifty-percent of the work performed by employees had virtually no correlation with enterprise value creation. While most people seemed to be doing their jobs well, there were systemic inefficiencies in achieving enterprise results.

With respect to individuals, consider the mid-level operations manager at a healthcare organization who laments about how fragmented his work has become, how he spends too much time dealing with new systems that are overly complex, and how internal consultants promoting lean-agile have actually created *more* work and *less* efficiency for his team. And consider the marketing professional at a direct-to-consumer firm who is frustrated with how much time she spends on contending with vast amounts of mostly unhelpful data, and how she spends too much time with instant messaging and in too many meetings on non-strategic issues rather than driving customer acquisition.

Knowledge work is based on the interactions between people and the flow of information to achieve specific outcomes that create value for customers and the enterprise. The root causes of low productivity are typically not driven by the lack of time, lack of data, lack of superstar performers, lack of new technology, or even the lack of technical or specialized know-how.

The root cause of the productivity problem is that knowledge workers spend too much time and effort not doing enough of the right things, or not being able to do them in the first place, due to unclear priorities, fragmented work, information overload, inefficient interactions, and poor processes. Moreover, team collaboration apps often makes things worse. Without strict regulation, digital technologies that intend to facilitate productivity can easily migrate from helping people work together to making it impossible for them to get their work done. McKinsey estimates we spend well over half our time doing emails and chat-messaging, and looking for information.

There are seven simple but powerful strategies that will help create a culture of productivity in almost any knowledge work environment. These strategies are interdependent, do not require expensive whiz-bang technology, and reflect the following underlying principle: as the external landscape increases in complexity and velocity, the more an organization's productivity drivers need to be elementary and foundational.

- **Synchronizing priorities:** Implement a strategy map that directly links work activity and outcomes to the drivers of enterprise results and value creation. Conduct periodic one-on-one and group check-ins to ensure that a few clear goals and priorities are understood and receiving the right level of attention. Openly discuss how to navigate the competing priorities of diverse stakeholder needs. As business conditions change, and strategy evolves, realign priorities and reallocate resources when necessary but avoid at all costs too many priorities and programs du jour.

- **Conducting conversations:** Openly discuss the importance and nature of productive conversations. Invest in developing interactive skills that lead to healthy and efficient conversations, emphasizing clarity of purpose, context, knowledge transfer, and desired outcomes. Reinforce that quality interactions are what build productive relationships. Implement an email usage protocol to reduce the time spent on and length of emails and other transactional messaging. Create efficient communication channels and facilitated norms within networks of activity.

- **Running meetings**: Reduce the number of meetings, standard meeting time, and total daily meeting time. Use a simple, disciplined methodology to conduct agenda-based and outcome-driven meetings. Whenever possible, do real work in the meeting, such as solving a problem, developing a recommendation, or making a decision.

- **Managing projects**: Implement a formal, disciplined, but simple project management methodology that is used on all project teams. Eliminate most project management dedicated roles and develop the capability across the workforce. Rigorously utilize project milestones and metrics, and assess outcomes in a highly disciplined manner. Reduce the number of formal, chartered project teams and manage remaining teams as a portfolio of assets.

- **Using data**: Prioritize and reduce the amount of information sent to people. Emphasize quality and not quantity of metrics, data, and analytics. The majority of information-sharing activity should focus on business model acumen: the drivers of cost, revenue, and productivity, including insights into acquiring and serving customers, along with relevant competitive intelligence. Eliminate analytics and reporting that are non-essential to strategy execution. Avoid following bandwagon trends like "big data" without a well-defined reason to do so. Streamline sources of data and information, clarify and make access user-friendly, and develop skills (not separate jobs) in efficient data mining and analysis.

- **Making decisions**: Reduce the cycle-time of most decisions. Develop and communicate a decision-rights matrix defining who makes what decisions. Keep decision-making groups small and decentralize decisions as deeply as possible into the organization. Reduce decision approval steps. Ensure decisions are not second-guessed outside of meetings, and are also effective, using periodic decision review sessions.

- **Optimizing work**: Eliminate most lean and agile dedicated jobs in the organization and develop lean and agile skills among knowledge workers to improve work design, reduce variances and bottlenecks, eliminate waste and non-value added activity, balance standard procedure with needed agility, and continuously improve key processes using a simple methodology. Periodically, require functional groups to conduct "work-out" sessions that enable them to stop doing low-value work, reduce fragmentation, and focus on whole work activity from beginning to end.

At an organizational level, there are several business processes that can be productivity killers for knowledge workers. These processes often cause widespread frustration and result in poor quality outputs that create further work. They include but are not limited to organizational budgeting, financial reporting, enterprise resources planning, and sales and operations planning. Knowledge workers often complain about these as too administratively burdensome and time-consuming, but what they are really saying is that these processes are not valuable enough in helping them do their best work to achieve results.

Consider the cross-functional initiative at a chemicals company to redesign the monthly forecasting and capacity planning process, with many suboptimal interactions among IT, sales, marketing, finance, and operations. The effort clarified a more disciplined procedure, reduced the cycle time of the process, streamlined the number of meetings and decisions, increased cross-functional collaboration, reduced animosity between functions, and improved the quality of both inputs and outputs such as inventory and working capital levels (all without adopting new technology).

Most organizations are confounded by knowledge worker productivity. They rarely have good definitions or metrics of productivity and often focus instead on knowledge worker engagement and satisfaction. While engagement and productivity are often correlated, a more direct and rigorous approach is needed.

Productivity is not primarily determined by an organization's strategy, business model, or use of capital and technology. The day-to-day behavior of people regarding how they prioritize their work, interact in groups and networks, exchange and process information, and solve problems and make decisions can build a culture of productivity and have a profound impact on improving knowledge worker productivity over the long-term.

Navigating and Leading Value Networks

Leading "frontier" firms are moving beyond value chains to value networks. As operating environments become increasingly interconnected, where work activities and processes span across traditional boundaries, organizations must shift their focus from a process orientation to that of a systemic network orientation. A value network represents a more reality-based construct of how people, activities, and assets inside and outside the organization must align, interact, and synchronize work to achieve desired results in a more optimal manner.

Supply chains are a misnomer, and are actually *delivery networks* that optimize the value drivers, such as asset utilization, cost, quality, and working capital, in the most productive manner to meet customer needs and achieve operating profit. The commercialization of new products and services is an example of a value network, requiring efficient interactions between many internal functions and external actors. Business processes, such as sales and operations planning, and customer relationship management, flow within and through these webs of activity.

Regardless of business model and operating model, aspiring leaders must learn to first navigate and then lead their enterprise value networks. Consider the financial services firm that is diversifying into broader service offerings as well as acquiring small firms to drive growth.

For the past few years, the firm has focused on improving core processes to drive profitability. As business model complexity has increased, along with the availability of beguiling new digital technologies, the company has made great efforts to keep things simple. It focuses on a critical few points of integration involving people, process, and technology as key drivers of value. With an increasing network orientation, the firm pays close attention to a) how processes must link with each other; b) where process flexibility vs. consistency is needed; c) where seamless transitions are required to drive both quality and efficiency in serving clients; and d) how productivity is measured and rewarded. As a result, during a period of growth and complexity, revenue per employee has consistently increased.

Both aspiring and experienced leaders today are embracing the network concept as the new way of thinking about structure, process, and value creation. There are *intra*-firm and *inter*-firm networks where value-creating activity spans across boundaries inside and outside the entity. The enterprise itself can be viewed as a value network, a web of relationships that generates value through dynamic exchanges between groups, functions, and other networks, both internal and external to the organization.

With this in mind, value network effectiveness can be explored based on network *dynamics*, network *capability*, network *productivity*, and overall network *effectiveness*.

Improving network productivity and effectiveness begins with understanding **network dynamics**:

- In our era of connectivity, work and the coordination of work occurs in formal and informal networks.

- Nodes in the network reflect places where there is value conversion: work activities are completed, information is converted into knowledge, and important decisions are made.

- Network nodes are connected to each other through relational links, or flows, using a variety of communications modes to exchange information, interact and collaborate, and convey work-in-process.

- Organization capabilities, people competencies, and cultural norms are distributed across the network, but not uniformly.
- Business processes often originate, terminate, and/or flow through one or more networks.
- Network performance is based on the quality and productivity of interactions that are coordinated to varying degrees, but often not formally facilitated or managed.
- The mindset of people often remains functional or process-oriented in nature, rather than network-driven.
- The lack of clarity and alignment of priorities, metrics, and incentives across the network is a common problem found in value networks that are under-performing.

Improving network productivity and effectiveness continues with building **network capability**:

- The enterprise shifts emphasis from linear processes and value chains to networked webs of activities and relationships that drive value.
- Intra-firm and inter-firm value networks are explicitly defined relative to their impact on capability-related outcomes: new product and service development, customer acquisition, revenue generation, and operating profit.
- Key value networks are examined to determine gaps between what the network is "designed" to deliver, what it is actually delivering, and what it needs to deliver.
- Value networks are formally resourced, managed and measured within a supporting organization system. Spanning across business processes, there are guided norms of interaction, work practices, and interfaces.
- There is alignment across the nodes and flows of the network with respect to how work is prioritized, information is shared, performance is measured, and incentives are used.

Given network dynamics and network capability, these diagnostic questions will help improve **network productivity**:

- How well are networks defined and clusters of network activity prioritized relative to their importance in executing strategy and driving value?
- How can the organization apply lean and agile thinking to the continuous improvement of network activity, emphasizing points of conversion: work that drives value?
- How can overall network design by simplified, streamlined, and synchronized to align priorities, focus work, and eliminate waste and non-value added activity?
- What new, critical few metrics and analytics need to be developed for increasing network productivity and linking those results to value creation?
- What are barriers to the quality and productivity of network interactions, information sharing, and decision-making?
- How can structure and hierarchical obstacles be reduced or redesigned to enable network performance?
- How can enterprise performance management and financial incentives better support network-driven work and cross-boundary collaboration?

Leaders in high performing organizations pay attention to the management and leadership of formal and informal networks. **See Diagram 6.** Elements of **network effectiveness** include:

- **Network facilitation:** A designated facilitator helps the flow of information and guides a user-friendly method for interacting and decision-making among network participants.
- **Network governance:** A regulating system helps monitor network activity to reinforce the quality and productivity of interactions and information exchange, and preserve the organic mode of the network. This includes measuring the performance of the network.
- **Norms of interaction:** Implicit and explicit norms of activity exist for sharing information, doing work, and using technology appropriately as a tool for interaction. These norms should be role-modeled by formal and informal leaders.

- **Network intelligence:** Processes and practices are used for managing information and learning as a total system so network ideas and knowledge are continuously updated.

- **Participation and composition:** Guidelines are used for the composition of the network, including who, how, and when people can join and participate. Some networks are managed almost as closed systems when it comes to membership, while others are open systems, while others have limited guidelines for membership.

- **Participant expectations:** There are expectations for the contribution of network participants relative to the purpose and goals of the network, the day-to-day intensity of activity in the network, the nature of roles and responsibilities, and the demonstration of network norms and behaviors.

- **Network interfaces:** A clear understanding of the points of connection within the network, the resource flows within the network and with other groups and networks, and the active monitoring and managing of the quality and performance of those interactions.

- **Performance management:** A method for measuring and assessing network performance through the facilitation and governance function supporting the network. Measures may or may not be defined in less formal networks, but there is a process for gaining participant observations regarding the usefulness and impact of the network.

Most networks are not intentionally designed or developed in much of a formal manner. They are emergent systems—in other words, they often emerge and evolve over time as series of activities that are interconnected but not well integrated.

With this in mind, even in small, less complex organizations such as an advertising agency, or a restaurant, leaders and their teams will perform better with a network orientation. Network awareness and attention will enable leaders to better understand, then navigate, then lead the moving parts of the enterprise ecosystem: customers, suppliers, vendors, partners, regulators, competitors, and communities.

NETWORK LEADERSHIP

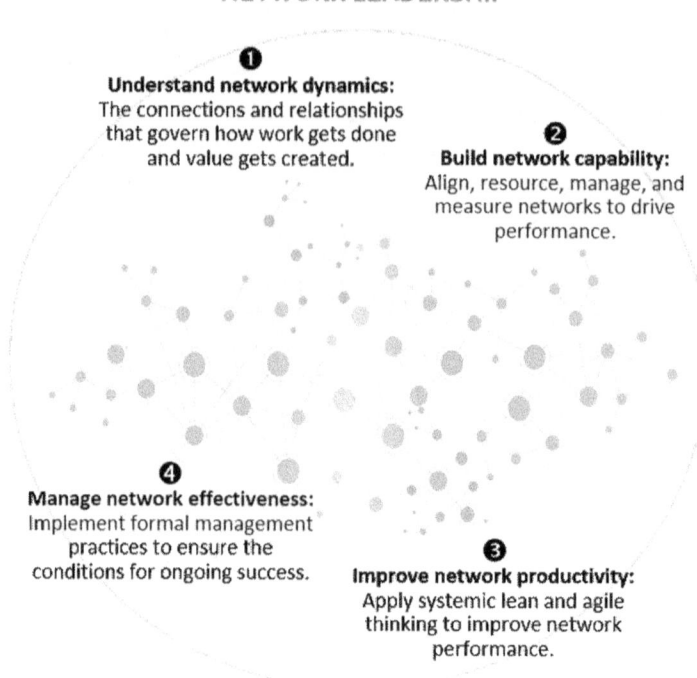

Diagram 6

In the case of a solo consultant and leader, consider the network she developed to grow revenue. She created a network diagram of current clients, target clients, key relationships, influencers, gatekeepers, buyers of services, and the web of connections between them. In a disciplined manner, every day she attempted to contact two or three people—nodes in the network—to share best practices, learn more about their needs, offer helpful support, and further connect people to each other.

Leaders should be mindful of certain "watch-outs" that indicate the need to improve network effectiveness. These include a lack of clear deliverables or outcomes from ongoing activity; a lack of interactive information exchange; a lack of true communication involving real forms of connectivity; an uneven distribution of focus and activity; the emergence of mini-webs or isolated islands within the network; and a lack of clarity of network composition, membership, and expectations.

To recap, in our digital and dynamic age, operations are often distributed across multiple firms, capabilities are spread across interconnected supply chains, specialized knowledge spans across loosely-defined alliances, relationships are developed with both collaborative and competitive channel partners, and complementary services are delivered by diverse providers. A cross-functional, cross-organizational network orientation is essential to long-term success in this new reality.

Measuring Total Productivity and Value Creation

While there is a productivity crisis overall, it is also true there are a number of leading firms that demonstrate a sustained ability to achieve much higher levels of labor productivity, return on invested capital, and profit.

How do they define, measure, and improve enterprise productivity? To be sure, many leaders and their firms will remain fixated on short-term revenue and profit jumps, often through highly inefficient but Wall Street-loving mergers and acquisitions, delivering big windfalls for the very few.

Recent research suggests their lifespans will be relatively short. However, the best firms that are truly committed to enduring value creation will continue to do the hard work of measuring real value for stakeholders over the long-term.

There are seven key enterprise-level productivity metrics that a leader should have a good working understanding of in measuring value creation. These supplement the baseline of balance sheet, cash flow, and income statement fundamentals.

- **Labor productivity**: Often used in organizations with substantial direct labor, this metric is more difficult to apply in complex organizations with large groups of knowledge-workers. It is defined as output over labor hours or output over labor investment, where output is either monetized or defined in terms of units. While challenging, this metric is an essential indicator of productivity for *all employee segments and for the enterprise as a whole*. The high performing enterprise achieves labor productivity levels that are greater than industry average and often increase over time.

- **Return on sales:** Operating margin is one of the most fundamentally sound return-on-sales metrics. It measures a company's margin health and operating efficiency. Similar to EBIT, operating margin is determined by operating profit divided by sales, where operating profit reflects sales revenue less cost-of-goods-sold and less sales, general, and administrative expenses. The high performing enterprise achieves operating margin levels that are greater than industry average and often increase over time.

- **Return on capital:** Also known as return on invested capital, ROIC measures how efficient a company is at allocating resources, and how well it is using money to generate returns. ROIC is determined by net profit less dividends divided by total capital. Similar to economic value added (defined below), a company is creating value when ROIC is greater than its weighted cost of capital, or WACC. The high performing enterprise achieves sustained levels of ROIC above its cost of capital.

- **Return on innovation:** Also known as return on innovation investment, this metric is used to evaluate how efficient a company is in new product and service development, and how well it is converting investments in R&D into additional profit. It is determined by comparing profit from new products and services to expenditures involved in their development and commercialization. The high performing enterprise achieves returns on innovation that typically correlate with ROIC and that increase over time, factoring out the effects of strategic (intentional) cannibalization.

- **Return on customer acquisition:** Related to customer lifetime margin or value, this metric can be used to assess how well a company uses resources in new product development, marketing, and sales to drive new customer profitability over defined time horizons. It is determined by comparing the total cost of acquisition to revenue or profit for specific customer segments. The high performing enterprise achieves returns on customer acquisition that increase over time for product and service families and customer segments.

- **Return on human capital**: Also known as return on human capital investment, ROHC measures how effective a company is in its human capital investments (it rightfully treats human capital expenditures as investments, not costs). It is determined by revenue less operating expenses less compensation, benefit, and training costs divided by either a) compensation, benefit, and training costs, or b) total number of full-time equivalents (FTEs). The high performing enterprise achieves human capital returns that are greater than industry average and often increase over time.

- **Economic value added**: Similar to return on capital, EVA measures a company's economic profit — the value created in excess of the required return of investors and debt-holders. It is determined by a company's net operating profit after tax (NOPAT) less its capital charge, where the capital charge is calculated by total capital times the weighted average cost of capital (WACC). Instead of net profit, NOPAT is considered a more accurate reflection of core operating efficiency without the influence of debt. The high performing enterprise achieves sustained levels of positive EVA: economic returns above a required rate.

It is easy to imagine how difficult it is to assess and compare productivity and value creation within and across industries. Obstacles to benchmarking include variations in definition, limited access to data, and limited availability of data due to the lack of attention to these metrics in the first place.

Therefore, firms that are serious about real value creation in the long-term will explore these metrics — perhaps even create a *productivity* or *performance index* that is integral to their strategy and scorecard — and establish their own internal baselines from which to improve upon over time. Sustained commitment to these critical metrics of success is a step toward differentiating from other firms. Enterprise earnings performance will follow.

Measuring enterprise productivity paves the way to *improving* enterprise productivity. The above metrics can be broken-down and linked to more forward-looking improvement metrics.

Here are a few examples of metrics that firms have used to drive real productivity improvement: killing potential new products more quickly (drives return on innovation); proportion of T&D investment in high-impact roles (drives return on human capital investment); decreasing the cost of high quality leads (drives return on customer acquisition); decreasing inventory levels for low contribution margin products (drives return on capital); and, proportion of G&A investment in value-adding versus transactional activities (drives return on sales).

In closing, the highly productive enterprise has a much better chance of survival and success due to competitive fitness, financial health, and sustained value creation. Leading firms pay much more attention to defining and measuring productivity at the enterprise level, avoid the trap of over-emphasizing individual or group efficiency, and perform significantly better than other firms with respect to returns on innovation, capital investment, and people.

CHAPTER 4
Culture and People

When it comes to culture, high-performing organizations create the conditions for groups of people to productively collaborate across organizational boundaries.

Chapter 4 - Culture and People

Introduction

This chapter explores selected topics in culture and people including the employee value proposition, performance management and people development; characteristics of high-performing, collaborative, and enlightened cultures; and, the elements of preserving and building culture.

As you read and think about this chapter, consider how your impact as a leader is linked to shaping and building culture within your team(s) and across the enterprise. Consider what is needed to effectively engage, inspire, develop, and reward people to do their best work in ways they find meaningful.

In exploring this chapter, consider a few questions: What aspects of culture and people will you strengthen or begin developing to grow as a leader? What new mindsets, behaviors, practices, and abilities are needed? What topics would you like to study further to deepen your understanding?

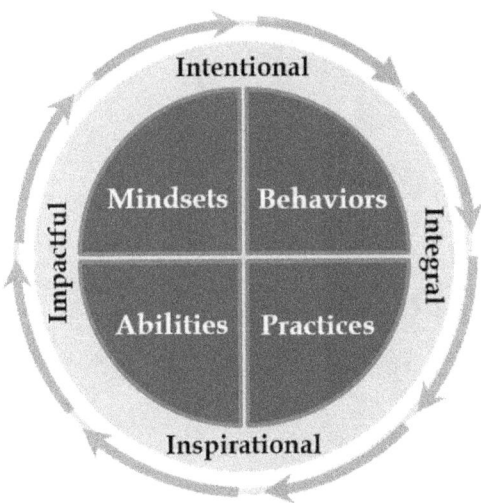

Diagram 1

Leaders can never underestimate the importance of culture in reaching sustained success. Culture is at the core of how people relate to each other and collaborate to get work done, which is the reason for being of every organization.

Unbundling the Employee Value Proposition

Every few years a major study confirms what most of us already believe and know: there is a strong link between employee satisfaction and enterprise performance.

But does employee satisfaction truly "drive" long-term, above-average enterprise performance? Exploring this question is not so much about the difference between correlation and causation, but rather, it is about whether employee satisfaction is actually a driver of value creation, or, is it more similar to value creation itself as an outcome of other factors. The answer depends on what is bundled within the definition of employee satisfaction and how it is measured.

Astute leaders are interested in employee satisfaction as a metric, but are even more interested in answers to related and more fundamental questions: Are people engaged in the strategy of the enterprise? Are they focused on the right priorities? Are they enabled to do their best work? Are they productive in achieving desired results? Are they having a meaningful employment experience? And, are the well-rewarded for their contributions?

Notice the emphasis here on things like strategy, work, productivity, meaning, and results. There is no question that employee satisfaction is desirable for many reasons. But given this, what should leaders really focus on and invest in with respect to culture and people?

Reviewing the basics, there are three drivers of sustained competitiveness and value creation: innovation, capital investment, and productivity. While indicators such as camaraderie, respect, and trust are related to satisfaction to some degree, none of them matter very much if they do not translate into performance and value. Organizations that achieve above-average value creation may have better employee satisfaction, but they almost always have the most collaborative culture and productive operations.

Organizations that thrive in the long-term establish a culture and value proposition that is in alignment with mission, strategy, business model, and the profile of people required to do the work and deliver results.

Every organization has a unique employee value proposition: what it offers people in return for their work. Elements typically include compensation and benefits, training and development, recognition and promotion, and work environment and affiliation. A compelling value proposition fits well with the mission of the enterprise and aligns with the needs and expectations of desired talent. It is integral to the evolving culture.

Leaders should review, invest, and reinforce their employee value proposition to address the most essential activities of how to best attract, engage, enable, reward, and retain the people needed for success.

When it comes to culture and the employee value proposition, high-performing organizations address a more foundational concept—either implicitly or explicitly—and that is productive collaboration. In this context, let's return to the question of what an organization should focus on with respect to its people to drive both performance and satisfaction. High-performing organizations pay close attention to strategic, smart, and specific investments in:

- **Health and wellness**: implementing practical mind-body-spirit health initiatives that help improve attention, promote mindfulness, reduce stress, eliminate bad habits, and increase overall energy levels.

- **Involvement and engagement**: mobilizing people in the strategy execution and value creation process to ensure ongoing clarity, focus, alignment, and commitment.

- **Relationships, teams, and networks**: creating the conditions needed for people to interact effectively and collaborate efficiently within an evolving organization structure.

- **Work design**: establishing roles, jobs, business processes, and work activities that reflect engaging degrees of challenge, flexibility, wholeness, creativity, and learning.

- **Performance management**: instituting a strong performance orientation through effective ways to set goals, prioritize work, share feedback, assess results, develop competencies, and continuously improve.

Chapter 4 - Culture and People

- **Financial rewards**: rewarding individuals and groups for their measurable contribution to value creation drivers (in a way that is internally consistent and externally competitive).

In an interesting case, consider how a large insurance company realized employee satisfaction was actually *too high*. While its operating margin had decreased significantly, employee satisfaction had increased to record levels. After in-depth diagnostic work, the organization found that employee satisfaction was too high among lower-performers and too low among high-performers. Moreover, there were too many low performers and too few high performers!

To revitalize the culture and improve results, it began a journey to strengthen its performance orientation through greater accountability, increase engagement through applied business acumen, and improve retention and attraction of needed talent through a refreshed value proposition. The main goal was to increase employee productivity for the long-term, understanding that, in the short-term, employee satisfaction would go down.

High performers are typically healthy, purpose-driven, fulfilled, *and productive*. They are engaged in meaningful work and inspired to do their best work. They are effectively supported by performance management, development, and rewards processes that align with their personal value proposition and support their contribution to results.

Employee satisfaction does not drive enterprise value. While there is a correlation, the factors of an organization's unique culture relate to investments in employee wellbeing, engagement, productivity, and rewards.

Improving Performance Management Impact

Most organizations and their leaders struggle with performance management. Leaders, managers, and employees alike perceive performance management as a burdensome program that delivers little value rather than as a business process that drives enterprise results.

However, high performing organizations and effective leaders have a very different perspective. They view performance management as a fundamental business process for driving the strategy execution of the enterprise. Performance management may be a misnomer; performance development is more accurate.

One of the best ways to develop leadership ability is to become a role-model in performance management for oneself and with others. Every organization has its own formal or informal performance management process, but the challenges with the process are almost universal:

- **Perceived as ineffective**: takes too much time, is tedious, and does not seem to make much of a difference.

- **Not a priority**: no real commitment from senior leadership as a process for "how the business gets managed."

- **Not relevant to how work gets done**: too much emphasis on individual performance and not enough on group.

- **Disconnected**: does not directly support or link with strategic goals and imperatives (unclear line-of-sight).

- **Event not a process:** it happens once a quarter or once a year and is not an ongoing process for useful dialog.

- **Too narrow of a focus**: is used only for determining a rating and making a pay decision.

- **Transactional:** too much emphasis on assessment and not enough on development and improvement.

Leaders do well to explore a few fundamental questions starting with: What is the purpose of performance management? How is it helping shape and create a high-performance culture? And how well is it working? Considerations for the purpose of performance management include a) developing talent, b) improving business results, and c) making reward decisions.

The most important leadership consideration for performance management is that it has the potential to be a core business process for building capability, shaping culture, and driving results. The most common mistake that leaders make is to limit

Chapter 4 - Culture and People

the possibilities of effective performance management from past experiences and outdated definitions.

There are several principles of performance management and development that are important for a leader to consider:

- The process is integrated with enterprise strategy execution and reinforces cross-functional goals and results.
- The process has a clear purpose of driving results, building capability, advancing people, and/or determining rewards.
- Line management, and not human resources, role-models and owns the process, responsible for its success.
- The process allows for some variation among employee groups based on the nature of role and work.
- Managers and non-managers are equally accountable for executing the process with quality.
- The process is designed for managing and developing the performance of average and good but not poor performers.
- Quality performance information is accessible to support robust goal-setting, feedback, and assessment.

Good conversations are the foundation of performance management and development. The quality of interactions between people in both formal and informal situations determines the degree to which people can communicate, coordinate work, and collaborate effectively. There are five main conversations that leaders in high-performing organizations become highly skilled at and utilize daily. Leaders should be intentional about learning and modeling these "crucial conversations" related to building rapport, setting expectations, sharing information, coaching improvement, and planning for growth. **See Diagram 7.**

Leaders can measure the impact of performance management. Potential metrics include leadership commitment to execution, accelerated goal achievement of teams, productivity of the workforce, engagement of the workforce, capability and bench strength of the workforce, return on investments in talent, and operating margins and revenue growth.

PERFORMANCE MANAGEMENT

The Five Key Conversations:
Building the relationship. Setting expectations and standards. Sharing performance information. Coaching and improving. Planning for growth.

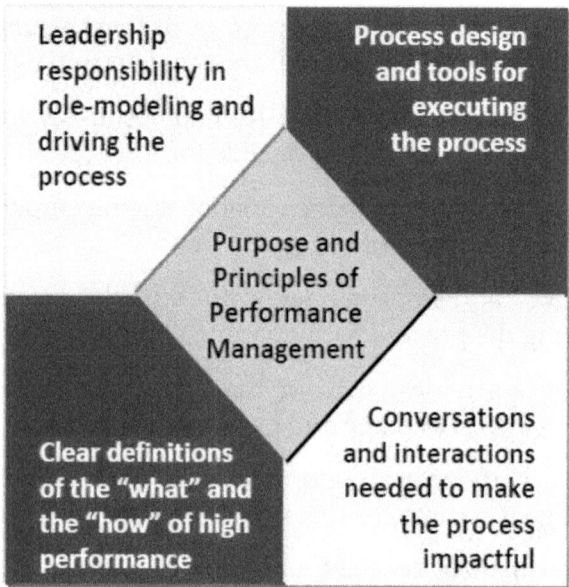

Most important consideration:
Performance management has the potential to be a core business process for building capability, shaping culture, and driving results.

Most common pitfall:
Past experiences with and current definitions can limit the creativity, scope, and potential for impact of the future process.

Diagram 7

Shaping a More Collaborative Culture

The new realities of organizations, their networks of activity, and their complex ecosystems are challenging leaders in almost every industry to rethink strategy, operations, and culture.

Market forces demand new value chains, business models, and operating models that require greater agility and speed. How work gets done is changing with formal and informal networks of people and small, nimble, coordinated teams that span across boundaries. Leaders are more distributed and must engage people in more open dialog and participative activity.

Barriers to change reflect the old ways of doing business: top-down planning, siloed functions, fragmented work, competing priorities, static resource allocation, slow decision-making, and misaligned incentives and rewards.

Facing these dynamics, leaders in a successful privately-held manufacturing enterprise developed new goals and priorities. *Strategic goals* focused on creating and commercializing new products and services, developing and growing new markets and customers, and making and delivering new products and services. *Organization priorities* focused on creating a productive and collaborative culture, building innovation-driven growth capability, and instilling human-centric design in a digital world.

At the center of this transformation, leaders identified the single-most important objective as: *creating the conditions for a more collaborative culture*. The senior leadership team developed the following principles for this mission:

- Create a shared understanding of business realities and a very open and honest assessment of enterprise needs.
- Support the space, time, and skills for having higher quality conversations about these realities and opportunities.
- Foster new mindsets, behaviors, practices, and abilities for more effective cross-functional cooperation.
- Eliminate unnecessary controls and protocols that block natural synergies from emerging.

- Utilize tools and technologies that facilitate productive and collaborative work activity.
- Implement shared goals, metrics, and rewards that span across traditional organizational boundaries.

Finally, the leadership team developed a strategy for preserving and strengthening culture while also transforming the business. Leaders agreed that bold, rapid, and sustainable transformation required a new and inspiring mission, the meaningful involvement of all managers in the change process, and the constant balancing of inherent tensions, opposing forces, and competing priorities, such as quality, cost, and speed.

Leaders agreed that a more productive and collaborative culture required a more productive and collaborative transformation process. Modeling a collaborative culture while building a collaborative culture was the key to success.

Exploring Enterprise Consciousness

As we enter the third decade of the new millennium our cultural, social, and economic landscape is dramatically evolving. People are more connected than ever before, new ways of organizing people are emerging, new values and belief systems are taking root, traditional boundaries are breaking down, webs of activity are more sophisticated, the laws of cause and effect are ever more confusing, and the degree of interdependence in the daily activities of our personal and professional lives continues to rise.

We are at the beginning of a new industrial age defined by the convergence of new eras in communications, social networking, cognitive technologies, energy conservation and generation, and environmental sustainability.

This new era has profound potential to ignite both innovation and productivity, the two most essential ingredients in the long run to the economic health of every enterprise. But there is a third and foundational ingredient in this mix — the element that will ultimately determine our collective destiny — and that is leadership and consciousness.

The concept of consciousness has many definitions, all of which point to a more expanded and enlightened awareness. In the context of organizations and the workplace, then, consciousness can be defined as the ability of an entity to transcend old patterns of thinking and behaving, expand its awareness of the nature of the world, and broaden its field of possibility in its operations and overall value creation efforts.

The primary problem is that most organizations and their leaders act and behave in *unconscious* ways, developing strategies and implementing operating models based on the harmful patterns of the old mechanistic, dualistic, and cause-and-effect view of the universe that has guided our socio-economic activities for centuries. These old patterns have helped create what has been termed by some as *unconscious capitalism*, and the consequences of this reality have become very clear over the past several years. It is in part why we continue to experience destructive industry bubbles, market swings and crashes, corporate scandals, environmental degradation, and brutal recessions.

There is no doubt that some organizations have made good progress in establishing elevated and enduring strategies, operating models, and cultures that enable them to achieve greater harmony with the changing environment and their evolving constituencies. These organizations are at the forefront of a change in direction and momentum toward a wholly different way of creating value through more conscious organizational activity and increased social responsibility. Consider, for example, the global technology services company that made available new software at no cost to researchers around the world fighting incurable diseases before the enterprise sold the software to customers. This organization has reinvented itself and achieved significant growth over recent years through smart innovation.

Unfortunately, however, most organizations have *not* fundamentally changed their beliefs or assumptions about how success should be defined in our highly interdependent world or what it takes to be sustainably successful and create value in an enduring and meaningful way. Consider, for example, the prominent retailing organization that, in an effort to change its overall cost structure, made across-the-board compensation and headcount cuts to its most expensive—*but also most knowledgeable and productive*—segment of its customer-facing workforce. This organization continued to act unconsciously, and unwisely, and died a slow, painful death.

An organization is not a sentient being, but there is tremendous value for aspiring leaders to think of an organization and workplace as a living, self-regulating system, a paradigm that is gaining traction as we learn more about the ecology of social systems. As organizations awaken and become more aware and wise, there are strong undercurrents of consciousness that flow within and through them.

The C-currents of shaping a more conscious culture include:

- *Curiosity*: Leaders ask a lot of questions. They seek to understand and learn new things. There is a climate of studying important topics deeply. There is a norm of sincere inquiry that counteracts the dangers of certainty and conformity. There are healthy, non-hierarchical, and open discussions.

- *Courage*: Leaders show courage through honesty. Leaders demonstrate daring, boldness, and resilience in creating the reality that will ensure enterprise survival and success within the dynamic ecosystem. Courage is the foundation for creativity, innovation, and constant transformation in a changing world.

- *Caring*: Leaders care about the perspectives, challenges, and needs of people. There is a clear sense of the ebbs and flows of the emotional climate within the workplace and how this climate affects the performance of individuals, groups, and networks. The health and wellbeing of people are viewed as essential to enterprise results.

- *Coherence*: Leaders shape culture over time. They establish the conditions that foster optimal work experience and consistent organizational norms for doing work. More effort is given to establish flexible working conditions that unleash creative and productive activity, and less effort to establish policies that coerce behavior through compliance.

- *Cadence:* Leaders establish a daily, weekly, and monthly rhythm for how the enterprise is managed. There is a disciplined consistency to key meetings, updates, reports, and other activities that are central to strategy execution and serving customers and other constituents.
- *Capability*: Leaders strengthen strategic and core capabilities on an ongoing basis. These capabilities reflect a unique mix of skills, knowledge, relationships, and processes across groups, networks, and the enterprise as a whole.
- *Collaboration*: Leaders reinforce healthy relationships by fostering highly collaborative and productive activities and interactions. Leaders pay close attention to collaborative work activity across functions and other boundaries.
- *Community*: Leaders create the conditions for building productive groups, networks, and communities. Interactions are grounded in the core values of honesty, curiosity, integrity, creativity, and unity. People easily interact, exchange ideas, do work, and form new relationships. As technology allows more work to be done virtually, leaders invest more, not less, in face-to-face collaboration.
- *Co-evolution*: Leaders understand that progress as an entity is interdependent with the evolution of the broader social and economic ecosystem and natural environment within which the enterprise exists. Leaders engage people at all levels to explore a wide range of opportunities for the future.

Like so many things, the consciousness of an enterprise begins with leadership. With respect to your own consciousness, in both life and work, think of it as a function of four elements: contemplation, connection, conversation, and creation.

Consciousness expands through *contemplation*—practicing deep introspection to increase self-awareness; through *connection* and *conversation*—engaging others in dialog and having meaningful conversations about important topics; and, through *creation*—learning and growing with others through the co-creative process of activities like developing new strategies, innovating new services, and exploring new markets.

Most organizations today have a sense of what direction they wish to be driving in, but have not yet awakened to a new, more conscious view of reality.

However, more leaders and their organizations around the world in both commercial and social sectors are walking a more conscious path. They are paving a more intentional road. They are acting more like organic systems than artificial organizations. They are breaking down centralized structures in favor of distributed networks. They are building new social networking and cooperative arrangements. They are investing in the health and wellness of their people. They are replacing control-based and fear-based management polices with inclusive and collaborative management practices. And they are recognizing their future is dependent on and inseparable from the consciousness out of which their actions originate.

Through increased awareness of reality, and a more enlightened view of our interconnected world, the conscious organization understands its own destiny is one that is shared with the destiny of its collaborators, competitors, customers, constituents, and communities alike.

Creating a More Enlightened Enterprise

There are clear differences between organizations whose leaders have helped them along the path of greater consciousness and those whose leaders have not. Here are several differences that are helpful to the leader in shaping values, norms, and culture:

- The unenlightened enterprise spends too much time talking about its values. The enlightened enterprise demonstrates its values in everything it does and spends more time talking about how its values translate into value creation.

- The unenlightened enterprise invests too much in detailed strategic plans that are intended to direct actions and behaviors, are often too complex, and are frequently obsolete by the time they are cascaded down the flagpole. The enlightened enterprise applies the power of strategic intent that creates the conditions for simple, focused, and flexible strategy development and execution.

- The unenlightened enterprise overemphasizes and over-engineers its compensation programs, often without the needed alignment across employee groups. The enlightened enterprise finds the right balance of financial and non-financial rewards, such meaningful work and development, to ensure a strong internal value proposition for its people.

- The unenlightened enterprise focuses too much on structure, often using organizational redesign as a lead strategy to improve performance. The enlightened enterprise invests less in structure change and more in the design and effectiveness of key capabilities, processes, and networks.

- The unenlightened enterprise can get obsessed with constant restructuring and reorganization that causes much disruption and discord. The enlightened enterprise focuses on putting in place simple practices and standard processes that drive better strategy execution.

- The unenlightened enterprise invests too much in the attention given to senior leaders based on hierarchy of role. The enlightened enterprise invests more in the development of leaders distributed throughout the organization based on the nature of role.

- The unenlightened enterprise overemphasizes succession planning at senior levels and underemphasizes talent planning for the workforce as a whole. The enlightened enterprise takes a systemic approach to ensure that across the organization the right people are in the right roles with the right skills at the right time and at the right price.

- The unenlightened enterprise treats middle-management as the main conduit for cascading information and implementing new things, and blames middle-managers when this does not go well. The enlightened enterprise replaces leading-from-the middle to leading from the periphery, where front-line customer-facing people lead change.

- The unenlightened enterprise hates uncertainty and narrows its field of possibility. The enlightened enterprise embraces uncertainty and broadens its field of possibility.

- The unenlightened enterprise puts too much emphasis on cool and trendy programs that are heavily-hyped and rolled-out with splashy fanfare. The enlightened enterprise makes small moves on a daily basis that make a big impact over time and quietly build a flywheel of improvement.

- The unenlightened enterprise pays too much attention to what competitors are doing. The enlightened enterprise pays much more attention to what customers are doing.

- The unenlightened enterprise does not trust non-senior leaders to make important decisions. The enlightened enterprise believes that well-informed employees close to the customer can and should make important decisions.

- The unenlightened enterprise invests too much in technologies for controlling internal processes. The enlightened enterprise invests more in technologies that enable it to evolve and drive growth.

- The unenlightened enterprise places too much emphasis on technology, confusing local efficiencies with total productivity. The enlightened enterprise takes a more strategic approach to the optimal combination of technology and people investments to drive systemic productivity and real value.

- The unenlightened enterprise often overutilizes formal teams that spend too much time in the forming and norming stages of their life-cycle and in unproductive meetings. The enlightened enterprise creates the conditions for teams to emerge and then dissipate organically based on dynamic needs.

- The unenlightened enterprise often demonstrates a stunning ignorance about health and wellness in the workplace, and will cast-out people who are struggling when it can. The enlightened enterprise understands the goodness in helping people who are unwell and in need of help to get better.

- The unenlightened enterprise expects executive leaders to manage, control, and coerce people into behaving certain ways. The enlightened enterprise expects executive leaders to role-model values-based behaviors and help create the conditions for others to do so as well.

- The unenlightened enterprise is defined by hierarchical power practices that are ego-driven and fear-based. The enlightened enterprise has a culture of low organizational drama where leaders are good stewards, and people are empowered to collaborate and do their best work.

Managing Idea Bombs from The Boss

A common challenge for managers and aspiring leaders is how to navigate seemingly unconscious idea bombs from the boss. Regardless of frequency or magnitude, top-down idea bombs can frustrate and confuse, affecting your ability to lead your own group and productively execute the work that matters most.

An idea bomb often comes from left field in a conversation or a meeting, where the boss might say something like *What if we...?* or *Why don't we try...?* followed by a suggestion that reflects a major change in direction. While usually well-intentioned, the incendiary device contributes to the main problem plaguing fragmented knowledge work today: scattered priorities and a lack of focus—wasting too much time, energy, and resources on the wrong things.

To be clear, creativity, flexibility, and agility are desired qualities in organizations for obvious reasons, and innovative ideas are worth exploring. But idea bombs are different. They burst onto the scene as a diversion from key priorities, requiring significant work that seems out of alignment with what is truly needed.

Consider the healthcare technology company where the new Director of Operations dropped an idea bomb with staff about professional certifications. "At my previous company, we had a number of certified scrum masters and black belts. Who wants to sign up?" While surprised at the invitation, within a day several team members were shifting workloads and schedules to fast-cycle outside training without a serious conversation about the rationale for the request and its resource implications.

There are situations when it makes sense to just do what the boss is asking. However, most idea bombs should not be blindly followed and can be handled in a way that is responsive to your leader while also best serving the organization. There are four types of good response frames, one or more of which you can deploy immediately after a random detonation, to respond effectively and role-model good practice with your own people.

The strategy frame: "The idea warrants consideration, there's real potential for value here. Can I ask a couple of questions, give it some thought in the context of our strategy and the business plan we are executing, and revisit it with you in a day or two?" This frame involves *evaluative clarity*: objectively assessing the idea relative to the drivers of desired results.

The diagnostic frame: "That's an interesting idea. Can you talk more about the impact you'd like to see and what might be required to do this? What are your thoughts on points of alignment with our current approach?" This frame involves *appreciative curiosity*: seeking to understand, listening to point out the positives, and probing with sincere questions.

The analytic frame: "That's a thought-provoking idea. Can we spend a few minutes exploring it further? Let's discuss desired outcomes, work required, resources involved, and fit with other priorities." This frame involves *careful discernment*: using thoughtful rigor to collaboratively make a decision that is informed by readily available evidence.

The capacity frame: "Great idea, but it most likely affects my ability to execute the plan we've put into place. Can I give it some thought, possibly circle back to you with questions, and then recommend how we might proceed?" This frame involves *situational agility:* applying experience to faithfully think through the dynamics involved and suggest the best course of action.

Consider the global professional services firm where the CAO dropped an idea bomb in a conversation with her VP of Talent Development. "Why don't we implement AI software to better connect networks of our people across regions?" The VP asked a few questions, requested a day to give the suggestion some thought, and came back to her with an alternative suggestion that fit better with current talent priorities: to first better understand pivotal roles, resource flows, and collaboration needs across existing networks.

An idea bomb from the boss can easily trigger your defense mechanisms. Be careful to avoid reactions like *We tried that before and it didn't work* or *It's a good idea, but we just don't have the time to do it*. Avoiding a defensive posture starts with an awareness that idea bombs are natural and expected, just unpredictable in terms of when and where they might drop.

There are also bosses who carpet-bomb, where big, disruptive ideas frequently come in clusters. In these cases, the four frames are useful, but may not be sufficient. In addition, you can utilize an operating framework, or even a strategy map, that clearly defines agreed-upon priorities and initiatives. An established framework may not prevent a new cluster campaign but can be very helpful in efficiently responding to it.

The four response frames are not mutually exclusive and share common principles. Each frame follows a pause and effect approach. They require your ability to pause, ask good questions, actively listen, and foster dialog in the context of key priorities. In applying one or more of the frames, you can resist immediate execution mode, and instead, offer a time frame and simple process for calibrating a direction together. These principles reflect fundamentals of managing up: good attention management and performance contracting.

Good leaders role-model a growth mindset through bold and innovative ideas. But there are times when ideas are idea bombs. When they explode, you can demonstrate mindful leadership through prudent pausing, deliberate consideration, and sound judgment to agree on a best path forward.

Reviewing the Elements of Culture

Culture can be defined as the beliefs, values, behaviors, and attitudes that characterize the social fabric of the enterprise and influence its daily functioning. A high performance culture that is meaningful to people—a value creation culture—is nurtured and created over time when the right people and conditions are present. A high performance culture emphasizes superior results, how to achieve results, how to best contribute to results, and how to prepare to sustain results in the future.

Leaders should never underestimate the importance of culture in driving sustained success. Culture is at the core of how people relate to each other and collaborate to get work done, which is the basic purpose of every organization.

Culture is enduring. It is impossible to replicate by competitors and survives the turnover of any one person. Good questions for any leader include: *What is our current culture? What is our desired culture? How can we shape culture? How will we get started?*

While every organization has a unique culture, there are common aspects of culture that leaders should pay attention to:

- The mission, brand promise, and values establish purpose: elevating reasons for why the organization exists.

- The employee value proposition establishes the reasons for why people join, stay, contribute, and find meaning.

- Leaders' style, language, and behaviors establish an expected code of conduct: norms for how people interact.

- Organization design and decision-making protocols establish formal and informal power structures.

- Performance management and improvement processes establish the performance orientation.

- Rituals, traditions, and celebrations establish a shared sense of history and community.

- Policies, procedures, and processes, with varying degrees of discretion, establish guidelines for how work gets done.

- Artifacts, symbols, and frameworks, ranging from logos to presentation templates, establish aesthetics.

- Facilities, equipment, and workspaces establish the quality of the physical environment.

- The people themselves, and their character and competency, establish the collective energy field of the enterprise.

CHAPTER 5
More Foundations of Leadership

True power comes from healthy self-empowerment: the development of a more conscious level of participation in one's life and work.

It reflects the ability to be fully aware, present, and useful in every situation. It comes from mind, body, and spirit wellbeing.

Introduction

This chapter further explores foundations of leadership including sources of power, leadership team development, and leadership paradigm development. The chapter includes several examples of mindsets, behaviors, practices, and abilities aspiring leaders have created to accelerate their growth in new roles.

As you read and think about this chapter, consider how your impact is linked to the impact of others. Consider how important it is to build a great leadership team that is unified, capable, and empowered, and how you are a role-model for those who are on their own leadership journey.

In exploring this chapter, consider a few questions: What are your sources of true power? What aspects of building team(s) will you strengthen or begin developing? What new mindsets, behaviors, practices, and abilities are needed? What topics would you like to study further to deepen your understanding?

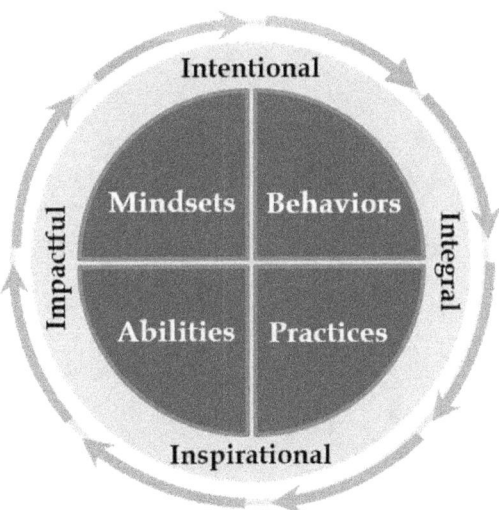

Diagram 1

Good leaders build good teams and great leaders build great teams. Effective leaders are first effective collaborators.

Understanding the Nature of True Power

Let's return to the definition of agency from Chapter 1 and the nature of authentic power: influencing and collaborating with others to achieve results in meaningful ways without overusing role-based authority or command and control behavior.

As you have probably already experienced, leaders often wield power primarily as a function of position based on status and hierarchy. This is not true power; it is more like artificial force and is ineffective in the long-run. One's position only opens the door to leadership opportunities.

True power starts with self-empowerment. Self-empowerment is the development of a more conscious level of participation in one's life and work. It reflects the power that comes from the ability to be fully aware, present, and useful in every situation. It comes from mind, body, and spirit wellbeing.

Self-empowerment is a state of being that comes from within and necessitates not giving one's natural power away. Consider these ways in which you can avoid giving others your power:

- When people disagree with your decision or direction, you can explain matter-of-factly without getting defensive.

- When people ignore key information and deny reality, you do not need to question your own thinking.

- When people try to manipulate you or push their agenda, you can respectfully say "no" and offer a better alternative.

- When people communicate aggressively or passively, you do not personalize it and can respond assertively.

- When people say things you don't believe, you can ask good questions, honor opinions, but act based on values and facts.

- When people act irresponsibly or make mistakes, you can look for your part in it but also hold them accountable.

Leaders own their power starting with the truth. True power begins with honesty and a commitment to reality. Leaders own their truth *and* are open to learning and changing their mind. They are comfortable saying *I don't know* and *I was wrong*.

Natural power sources enable leaders to guide activities and achieve results in ways that establish respect, build trust, and inspire others to do their best. The P-model of true power is:

- **Principle** is a source of true power. Principle reflects a deep commitment to demonstrating your values in all situations.

- **Purpose** is a source of true power. Purpose reflects how intentional and mission-driven you are in your role.

- **Presence** is a source of true power. Presence reflects mindful awareness and attention without imposing judgment.

- **Priority** is a source of true power. Priority reflects how planful you are in focusing on the things that matter most.

- **Passion** is a source of true power. Passion reflects the positive attitude, vitality, and energy you bring to your work.

- **Perspective** is a source of true power. Perspective reflects the ability to expand awareness and keep things in proportion.

- **Preparation** is a source of true power. Preparation reflects your groundwork and degree of readiness for key activities.

- **Proficiency** is a source of true power. Proficiency reflects the depth and breadth of competency you demonstrate.

- **Patience** is a source of true power. Patience reflects the art of pausing and the willingness to slow down when necessary.

- **Perseverance** is a source of true power. Perseverance reflects your strength of conviction, determination, and resilience.

One more source of true power is **Compassion**. Compassion is about leading from both the head and heart. The compassionate leader *never* denigrates, manipulates, or humiliates people. She knows cruelty is weakness and compassion is strength.

The compassionate leader cares about the wellbeing of self and others. She is kind, thoughtful, and respectful. She is attentive to the needs of others, and recognizes and relates to their situations, but does not allow their distress to transfer back to her. She is generous with time when helping her teams learn and grow while also holding them accountable to high standards.

Chapter 5 - More Foundations of Leadership

To reinforce these sources of authentic power, consider the case of a program manager in a consumer products company. After several years of establishing his reputation as a leader with strong principle, presence, performance, perseverance, and compassion, he developed a new paradigm to accelerate growth and become more promotable.

This leader was known for getting things done, following through, and helping others. He was considered *the* source of institutional knowledge for a specific product family. He had a history of delivering on his commitments and being a great collaborator with strong values. But he had not advanced to his satisfaction and often found himself acting with fear and anxiety.

He started on a personal mission of self-empowerment that involved the development of a new leadership paradigm and growth plan. After several conversations with colleagues, internal customers, other leaders, and a coach, he decided to focus on the power sources of purpose, priority, preparation, and proficiency.

He identified a new *mindset* to become more strategic. He became more purposeful in linking strategy and operations, and more proactive in engaging with senior leaders about improving strategy execution to drive revenue and profit. He identified a new *behavior* to migrate from passive to assertive and combine a "How can I help?" attitude with a "This is what we need to do, and this is why" approach. He identified a new *practice* to better prepare for recommending new courses of action rather than just executing plans or responding to requests. And he identified a new *ability* to publicly communicate more clearly and persuasively with leaders and groups on strategic topics in both formal and informal settings.

Another key aspect of the leader's paradigm was his dedication to a very healthy lifestyle with commitment to mental, physical, and spiritual fitness. He was a role-model in leading himself and enjoying a balanced and integrated work-life with high quality relationships. He recognized the importance of perseverance in following through on his plan, working with a coach, letting go of old, limiting beliefs, and developing new ways of thinking, being, and doing. He was promoted within a few months.

Perhaps more than anything, power is a state of mind, and so self-empowerment also begins with one's mindset. Building on the popular growth-mindset paradigm, leaders can replace old mindsets with new ones, using these frame-changers:

- Having conversations about new ideas: **Stop** listening with this frame: Is it right? Do I agree? **Start** listening with this frame: What does it mean? What can I learn?

- Staying humble when tough surprises come along: **Stop** using this frame: Why is this happening to me? I don't deserve it. **Start** using this frame: What is happening? What were the forces that caused it? What can I learn?

- Avoiding taking things personally: **Stop** feeling responsible for what other people think, say, and do. **Start** being responsible for what you think, say, and do.

- Waiting for things to happen or get done: **Stop** being agitated or frustrated because you feel time is wasted. **Start** observing, reflecting on, and appreciating everything around you.

- Building a solid foundation for long-term impact: **Stop** trying to make quantum leaps with quick and easy big wins. **Start** making small moves that build on each other, make a big difference, and lead to lasting results.

- Dealing with a multitude of urgent needs: **Stop** responding right away to all inquiries and requests. **Start** putting some time and space between actions and reactions.

- Handling difficult situations: **Stop** trying to fix everything that is broken or solve every problem. **Start** letting more situations unfold fluidly and resolve themselves.

- Collaborating within diverse teams: **Stop** focusing on how people are different and what we disagree on. **Start** focusing on what we have in common and what we agree on.

- Managing the busyness of daily life: **Stop** forcing things, acting with urgency and certainty, and rushing around. **Start** being active but also at ease, intentional but also relaxed, and leave early to arrive early to meetings.

Developing the Leadership Team

Good leaders build good teams and great leaders build great teams. Leadership is a team sport. Effective leaders are effective collaborators and teammates first.

Building good or even great teams involves hiring the right people into the right leadership jobs, building relationships and trust with team members, emphasizing alignment among team members on a daily basis, actively using a set of operating principles, and managing and developing the performance of the team and team members. **See Diagram 8.**

Consider the following set of operating principles that a leader at a consulting services company co-developed with her leadership team comprised of functional leaders:

- **External and strategic focus**: We will stay strategic and externally-focused and build an integrated organization.

- **Clarity and alignment**: We will define and communicate clear goals and aligned priorities for each of our teams.

- **Enterprise orientation**: We will be collaborative, non-territorial, and unified in leading the organization.

- **Functional excellence**: We will succeed through others by providing direction, expertise, support, and guidance.

- **Shared values and norms**: We will strive to preserve a culture of respect, empowerment, quality, and productivity.

- **Collaborative relationships**: We will meet regularly, learn from each other, and assess our progress in order to improve.

- **Disciplined execution**: We will continuously improve core business processes to relentlessly drive results.

- **Mutual accountability**: We will develop abilities as individual leaders and as a team and help each other succeed.

Building leadership team capability requires active team performance management. The same leader above used a quarterly process to ask for feedback from the team, share key themes, and openly discuss team-building opportunities.

Empowered Leadership

LEADERSHIP TEAM EFFECTIVENESS

Diagram 8

A useful set of questions for this team-based performance management and development process included:

- Given our operating principles, what is currently working well as a team and what are some of our strengths?

- What is currently not working so well, how is this affecting our performance, and why do we think it is happening?

- What can we do to create greater day-to-day alignment? What behaviors need to stop, start, or continue?

- What mindsets, skillsets, and toolsets do we need to focus on to become more effective as a team of leaders?

- How will we do all of this while also making our personal experience meaningful and fulfilling?

Over time the rules of *make it clear, make it real, make it work,* and *make it last* became a standard operating procedure for the leadership team. And their teams effectively prioritized, aligned, and integrated work activities across the function to manage natural tensions and achieve their goals.

Harmonizing Natural Tensions

Leaders effectively navigate competing priorities and opposing forces — the natural tensions of management. In the spirit of equanimity and agility, they manage the predictably unpredictable stress and pressures that combine, interact, and then dissipate in our dynamic world. Things fall apart, come together, and then fall apart again. Progress is almost always iterative with wrong-ways, detours, and dead-ends.

In the marketplace there are the obvious dynamics of supply, demand, barriers to entry, barriers to exit, and competitive disruptions. In their networked ecosystems, organizations are often challenged with the shifting terrain of social, economic, environmental, legal, and political forces. But there is also a shifting terrain in the organization itself.

Within the enterprise, leaders and their teams are faced with priorities, tensions, and forces that compete for managerial attention and resource allocation. A useful way to reflect on this dynamic involves the concept of co-existing pairs. Leaders are often challenged to harmonize these common dualities: clarity *and* flexibility; focus *and* growth; productivity *and* quality; volume *and* speed; standardization *and* service; innovation *and* efficiency; old *and* new technologies; aging workers *and* new hires; and, managing costs *and* making investments.

Consider the case of a for-profit orthopedic surgical practice with several physician-partners, multiple locations, and over one hundred employees. At a three-day off-site of the leadership team, leaders landed on two co-existing pairs that had not been obvious as a pair but were critical for success. The first pair was productivity and patient satisfaction. The team developed several priorities for increasing collaboration across departments while also improving the quality of the overall patient experience. The second pair was less patients and more revenue. The team developed a second set of priorities for specializing in certain client segments while also introducing an innovative treatment approach to increase revenue per ideal patient.

The co-existing pair concept is useful at the individual leader level as well. Consider the head of engineering at a custom fabrication company. This leader created a development plan to become more strategic and more relational. While an excellent tactician, he identified new behaviors for achieving greater balance in direction-setting *and* process execution. While very transactional, he identified new practices for staying efficient *and* building stronger relationships.

Organizations do not exist in an either-or world. In navigating the shifting terrain, leaders must work together to creatively solve problems in ways that better align and balance internal and external network energies that are often disparate in nature. While strategic and core capabilities are essential as the key areas of emphasis, leadership is also an exercise in finding the intersections where many different forces converge.

Managing the Football Not the Hockey Stick

Continuous flow can be applied to the management of project work. Recall we are inclined to perceive life and work as a series of discrete experiences without our full attention to the in-between. In this context, rather than focusing on a single, event-driven deadline, leaders can manage work along a roadmap of progress milestones and check-ins.

In a continuous flow environment, work on each project can be graphed as a flattened normal distribution, resembling the upper half of a football, where most activity is executed in the middle of the timeline and with thoughtful preparation up-front and needed quality review later on. Unfortunately, in many organizations, work is not done this way, and when graphed, looks more like a hockey stick with the blade pointed up. Most activity is pushed off until the deadline nears and then spikes dramatically with people scrambling to get things done and with little time for quality review or impact analysis.

Chapter 5 - More Foundations of Leadership

Consider both the transportation company and the behavioral health non-profit that adopted the football strategy across their portfolios of projects. Leaders found that the flow approach to managing projects and project teams eliminated the finishing frenzy at the end and reduced the number of projects that got dropped, delayed, or reprioritized. Moreover, there was greater concentration and focus, less multi-tasking and lower switching costs, and higher levels of both quality and productivity. Work groups were able to better manage unknowns, respond to surprises, and reduce overall stress and burnout.

Managing work like a football and not a hockey stick does not require any more planning or resourcing. It is simply a strong commitment to work differently. In a portfolio of projects, when several football-shaped graphs are staggered and overlaid on one another, there is a continuous, manageable, and steady level of activity. Conversely, when several hockey stick-shaped graphs are overlaid on one another, there is a continuous turmoil of last minute spikes in activity, one after the other.

A good way to further compare the two approaches is to put them in the context of college. Imagine you are back at the university with a course load of four major classes, but this time as a leader of teams, one team per course.

In the hockey stick approach, teams do very little work—the bare minimum—during the semester and then cram for exams at the end and pull all-nighters to finish projects with very little time for you to provide guidance or review for quality. If any surprising challenges arise, you would find yourself in the professor's office begging for extra time with your grade at risk.

In the football approach, each team reviews the course syllabus with you, develops a high-level roadmap with milestones, completes all work when it is assigned, and prepares all assignments for review with you before turning them in. Studying for exams and completing key projects are done several days in advance of deadlines. You and your teams would be relaxing at the corner tavern the night before finals, where some team members might even comment that they have already started reviewing the new syllabi for next term.

Using Precise Language in Communication

Clear communication is critical for good leadership. Unclear communication, or miscommunication, is a key obstacle to the leader's ability to guide the coordination and collaboration needed for effective strategy execution.

An often-overlooked ingredient in the recipe for good communication is the use of a common language. Most of us would agree that enterprise life is plagued with trendy jargon and the lazy application of words that can mean many different things. For example, consider how organizations constantly struggle with the differences between *goals*, *objectives*, and *priorities*.

Leaders at all stages of their growth curve pay attention to language and are very intentional in how they use words and concepts in influencing teams, functions, and organizations. There usually is no "right" definition for, or application of, a term. The key is to be precise and consistent—highly intentional—in the use of important terms. Here are a few to be mindful of:

- **Mission, vision:** mission typically reflects the purpose of the enterprise; vision reflects a future scenario of success.
- **Strategy, imperative, initiative:** strategy is more general and directional, while strategic imperatives and related initiatives are more specific and detailed.
- **Customer, consumer:** customer is any payer in the value network; consumer is the end user of the product or service.
- **Goal, objective, priority:** goal is more broad in nature while priority is more narrow, and objective can be used in place of one or the other.
- **Role, job:** role typically reflects a level of jobs, such as mid-management; job reflects a specific position.
- **Responsibility, accountability:** responsibility pertains to job duties; accountability pertains to key results.
- **Skill, competency, ability:** skill is more specific while competency is a bundle of skills, knowledge, and behaviors; and, ability can be used in place of one or the other.

- **Policy, procedure, process**: policy requires specific behavior; procedure provides specific steps of work; and, process guides people in carrying out bundles of work.
- **Efficiency, productivity**: efficiency reflects outputs relative to standards; productivity reflects outputs relative to inputs.
- **Observation, assessment**: observation reflects objective information; assessment reflects subjective judgment.
- **Outcomes, results, value**: outcomes are often qualitative, results are often quantitative, and value is impact delivered to stakeholders, such as customers.

Again, the most important practice here is less about using the terms correctly, although they should be used accurately, but rather that leaders and their teams are intentional about how terms are consistently used and clear about *exactly* what they mean.

Creating Your Leadership Paradigm

Recall that core responsibilities are the basic activities of a leader at any level, proven practices are the universal attributes of effective leaders, and enlightened competencies are the skills and behaviors that wise leaders often demonstrate.

Along with other leader characteristics shared in this book, we can distill these different lenses into a blueprint, or pathway, of eight collaborative leadership actions:

- Leaders co-create a vision that is elevating and challenging for their team(s).
- Leaders translate the vision and mission into a compelling strategy about what to do and what not to do to serve customers and create value.
- Leaders recruit, on-board, engage, develop, and reward people in meaningful and fulfilling ways.
- Leaders empower people and create the conditions for them to do their best work.

- Leaders actively measure milestones and results, openly sharing performance information and feedback.
- Leaders foster a growth mindset by creating safe spaces for creativity, innovation, experimentation, failing, and learning.
- Leaders emphasize mind-body-spirit balance and wellness with themselves and others.

Empowerment can be defined as creating an environment where people are given the resources to make decisions, and the freedom to actually decide, about how to best do their work within broad but clear boundaries. Here are seven strategies for leaders at all levels to empower people:

- Be clear about job performance expectations, desired work behaviors, and important cultural norms.
- Give people the discretion to do their work using tools, protocols, and processes that they help to create.
- Encourage experimentation and openly talk about failures and successes in the spirit of continuous improvement.
- Give people access to real-time performance information and the elbow-room to act on that information.
- Engage people to participate in important problem solving and decision-making, especially as they relate to customers.
- Be approachable: show an openness, willingness, and patience to slow down and have quality conversations.
- Let people know they matter during the day-to-day activity and be clear about how their work contributes to success.

Leader impact has two related dimensions: what is achieved and how it is achieved. The "what" pertains to the results of the leader's group(s). The "how" pertains to the ways in which those results were achieved, relating to values, behaviors, and norms.

Chapter 5 - More Foundations of Leadership

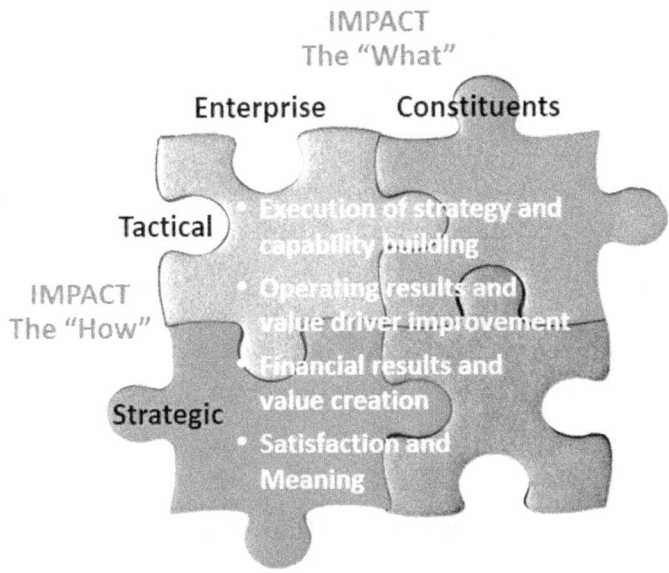

Diagram 9

As leaders advance in role, and progress in capability, their rubric for success broadens to reflect outcomes from a greater diversity of internal and external stakeholders. The aspiring leader should think of impact from the perspective of self, boss, team, enterprise, and customers (and other external stakeholders and constituents). **See Diagram 9.**

After giving some thought to impact, you can begin developing a formal leadership paradigm. The paradigm is meant to be a living, evolving 1-2 page document, often framed as a set of principles that will guide you on a daily basis. **See Diagram 10.**

Here is an action plan to develop your leadership paradigm and growth plan (which you might work on with a coach or mentor):

- Develop a one-to-two page leadership paradigm, or strategy, as a set of guiding principles that reflect key mindsets, behaviors, practices, and abilities for the next year. Develop 2-3 bulleted principles for each of these four elements.

- Write your paradigm in a way that you can either read or explain to your team(s). Share it with them. Emphasize mindsets and behaviors: your beliefs, values, and desired ways of being—how you will show up as a leader.

- Develop a leadership checklist of high-performance habits and practices that reflect ways in which you will manage self and manage work. Emphasize the routines you will follow to integrate work-life for mental, physical, and spiritual health.

- Develop a growth plan with indicators of progress and metrics of success. Emphasize the strengths you wish to build-on and new abilities you wish to develop. Include how you will be intentional, integral, inspirational, and impactful.

Consider this excerpt of guiding principles from the paradigm of an aspiring leader who was new to leading a function:

- My leadership paradigm has four pillars: engage, empower, inspire, and appreciate

- I *engage* people through active listening and undivided attention. I *empower* people by supporting stretch assignments that create growth experiences. I *inspire* people by consistently role-modeling positive attitude and truth-telling. I *appreciate* people by using sincere, specific, and frequent feedback.

- An obstacle to strategy execution is lack of alignment across groups. To close this gap, I will openly share information and break down silos through shared goals and rewards.

Here are three more real-world examples of leadership principles from leaders who are new to their roles. Again, notice the integration of new ways of thinking, being, doing, and working to be more intentional, inspirational, and impactful.

- **Partner at a financial planning firm**. This leader was challenged with building internal operating systems to improve efficiencies while targeting a more ideal profile of clients to grow revenue. Patience and resilience were required as he worked with independent-minded senior partners to establish a cadence to managing the firm in a more collaborative and disciplined manner. New practices consisted of weekly operating calls, monthly performance meetings, and quarterly strategy sessions. Knowing there would be passive resistance, he adopted this paradigm principle: *Progress does not happen in straight lines. There will be ebbs and flows in interest and commitment. Over the next year, the partners will experience the value of these interactions and gradually begin to support them. I will stay resilient.*

- **Principal at a private high school.** This leader was challenged with building a new administrative team to lead the school and both manage and collaborate with faculty to best serve students, families, and the community. Openness and transparency were required as she worked with administrators and teachers to steadily establish mutual rapport, build trust, set direction, and prepare for new initiatives in the coming year. Knowing there was a lack of capability early on, along with a natural fear of failure, she adopted this paradigm principle: *We will share information, discuss direction, and work together to create new programming and change culture. I will consistently reinforce the co-existing pairs of preserving the core while investing in the future, and breaking down silos while maintaining department specialization and identity.*

- **Manager at a family-owned business.** This leader was challenged with developing new business to grow revenue in a small company that had several family members in leadership positions. There were typical dynamics involved, including how to best keep personal and business matters separate, and how to find common ground among enmeshed but very different personalities. Skillful priority and boundary management were required as he worked to ensure that family member perspectives were represented while implementing new client acquisition processes that would expose the natural tensions of preserving margins and investing in the future. Knowing there was a lack of understanding about on-line and social media go-to-market strategies, he adopted this paradigm principle: *We will explore new strategies together with just enough education to help leaders make good decisions as a team. I will be assertive in resisting the second-guessing of decisions but will openly review results on a regular basis to address concerns and make adjustments.*

PARADIGM DEVELOPMENT

Element	Description	Examples
Mindsets and Behaviors	Your values and beliefs about life and work and leadership. How you think about and approach your work. The mental models you use to stay centered and be effective. How you consistently want to show-up. The effective behaviors for leading people and managing work. The ineffective behaviors to watch out for and avoid.	There is no failure, just opportunities to learn. When you see a problem, always bring a solution. Do less to achieve more. Effective behavior of seeking to understand in active listening. Ineffective behavior of moving away from people under stress.
Practices and Abilities	The habits and skills you leverage and develop to be effective. The work practices required to gain and sustain traction in your role.	Commit to two hours Friday afternoon to reflect on week ending and beginning. Build financial analysis skills.
Leadership Impact	The qualitative indicators of progress and success including milestones. The quantitative metrics of impact and results that are relevant to your role. Your rubric of success in terms of the what and the how.	Increase in stakeholder satisfaction and success. Redefine impact as results through teams with both operational and financial metrics.
Integrated Work-Life	How you integrate work and life for sustainable health and wellness of you and family. How you create an integrated self: intentional, integral, inspirational, impactful.	Will limit work on the weekends to 2 hours. Will do daily mind-body-spirit health and wellness practices with discipline.

Diagram 10

Imagining the Senior Leader Paradigm

As a young leader, you may aspire to be the senior executive one day. A good way to plant seeds for the future is to imagine a set of questions and considerations that are important to the top executive after years of leadership experience.

Whether the chief executive of a company, the managing partner of a firm, the senior leader of a business unit or division, or the founder of a new venture, ongoing development involves navigating the dynamics of strategic, organizational, and personal challenges of daily work and life. This is not all that different from the early days of your first leadership role.

The difference perhaps is the level of sophistication of the questions and the breadth of stakeholders to which they refer, which is what makes them useful as you develop your own leadership paradigm and style. Leadership does not happen overnight. Thinking about what's important to the senior leader of the future will help you in your leadership development now. How might you begin viewing leadership as systemically as a General Manager or Chief Executive Officer?

Someday, maybe soon, you may earn the privilege of leading an enterprise. As you think about the future, the integrity *and* integration required of leadership, and the opportunity to inspire others and make an impact, consider these ten good lines of questioning for a senior executive leader:

- **To what extent is the strategy clear, compelling, and discerning?** How focused and resourced is the organization to achieve a critical few strategic goals and business priorities. Related questions include: How clear is the mission? How bold is the strategy in defining success and the drivers of success? How differentiated is the value proposition in the marketplace? How is the firm preserving and building sources of competitive advantage? How is it evolving with the external global environment?

    Leadership practice: *Great leaders create a positive energy field and hope about the future.*

- **To what extent is the leadership team aligned, committed, and capable?** How ready and prepared is the senior leadership team to lead the enterprise? Related questions include: Are leaders unified and consistent in how they are engaging the organization? Are they demonstrating functional excellence while also actively creating a team-based, enterprise orientation? Are they disciplined in investing in their own development as a team and as individuals? How strong is your relationship with the leadership team and how might it be strengthened?

    Leadership practice: *Great leaders build great teams that are unified, capable, and empowered.*

- **To what extent are leaders effectively communicating, collaborating, and coordinating?** How well are leaders teaming to execute strategy within their functions and across boundaries? Related questions include: Are leaders preventing and breaking down functional silos? Are they demonstrating values and norms that shape the desired culture deep into the organization? Are they effective at resourcing, guiding, communicating, and supporting key initiatives? How might your leadership approach need to change to further reinforce the desired culture?

    Leadership practice: *Great leaders consistently emphasize three frames: strategy, people, and culture.*

- **To what extent is the enterprise achieving desired business results and creating value?** How well is the organization achieving strategic goals in ways that deliver value? Related questions include: How well is the organization performing relative to lead indicators and key metrics? How well are these aligned with financial incentives? How well is the organization managing its product and service portfolio to grow margins? How well is the organization balancing short-term results with long-term investment?

    Leadership practice: *Great leaders understand the business and reinforce reality with their team.*

Chapter 5 - More Foundations of Leadership

- **To what extent is the enterprise improving in key value generating activities?** How good is the quality and productivity of the organization? Related questions include: How is the organization eliminating systemic cost and waste and increasing operating margins? How productive is the organization in innovating and commercializing products and services? How productive is it in developing and growing markets and customers? How productive is it in making and delivering products and services? How well are technology and data platforms serving strategy execution without disruption?

    Leadership practice: *Great leaders focus on real productivity to drive margins and value creation.*

- **To what extent is the workforce engaged, inspired, and enabled to do their best work?** How impactful are talent management and other workforce processes? Related questions include: Are people focused on doing the work that matters most—that drives business results and creates value? Are they able to do their work productively with minimal bureaucratic obstacles? Is the firm effectively attracting, deploying, and developing talent in a strategic manner? Are leaders demonstrating positive behaviors in visible ways that energize people around serving customers, realizing mission, and creating value?

    Leadership practice: *Great leaders create the conditions for people to do their best work.*

- **To what extent is there a good working relationship with the board or parent?** What is the quality of the relationship between senior leadership and directors or owners? Related questions include: Is the board or ownership team operating at the proper strategic altitude and clarity in governance? Are your communications balanced with desired degrees of transparency, directness, and flexibility? Are you proactively building relationships and trust with board members?

    Leadership principle: *Great leaders are highly ethical and play the long game.*

- **To what extent are you performing your role effectively with respect to stakeholder expectations?** Is there a comprehensive definition of performance and growth given the reality of competing priorities? Related questions include: How well are you meeting or exceeding the expectations of customers, owners, shareholders, partners, alliances, and communities in which the enterprise operates?

    Leadership practice: *Great leaders embrace and demonstrate a growth mindset.*

- **To what extent are you realizing your desired purpose, meaning, and fulfillment?** How well is the leader's personal value proposition being fulfilled? Related questions include: How balanced are your responsibilities with respect to mindshare, time, and effort, and how is your perspective evolving? What do you find most rewarding in your work? How fulfilled are you regarding your own personal growth and professional development? How do you feel about the reputation and legacy you are building for the long-term?

    Leadership practice: *Great leaders are authentic: honest, open, transparent, and vulnerable.*

- **To what extent do you have a vision for the future?** What are the leader's future goals and plans? Related questions include: What are your goals for the future with respect to your current role or other roles of interest? What is the succession strategy and plan for your role? How transparent does this plan need to be? What other experiences are you interested in over the next few years for your career, desire for impact, and legacy?

    Leadership practice: *Great leaders live a clear personal mission and are very fit in mind, body, and spirit.*

Closing

Leaders do not need to be superheroes, but they are heroic in their humanity and self-empowered to help others succeed. They are people too with imperfections like everyone else.

Developing a leadership mindset starts with your beliefs about the world of work and people. Kevin Cashman, a leader in executive development, has said, "Beliefs are the software of leadership, our personal operating system that runs the show." Beliefs create our reality as the lenses and filters we use to process information, make sense of things, and take action.

One of the big challenges aspiring leaders face in becoming empowered is overcoming self-limiting fears and beliefs. These are the storylines our minds create. Consider the conscious belief that "I am committed to excellence" combined with the often unconscious belief, lurking below the surface, that "I am not good enough." Remember, you are not an imposter as a leader. When a limiting thought arises, see it, feel it, then let it go.

Your ability to reframe self-limiting notions will come with increasing your breadth and depth of experiences, expanding your perspective, and becoming comfortable with uncertainty.

There are three common forms of self-sabotage that stem from fear and anxiety among new leaders: personalization, procrastination, and perfectionism. Reflect on how you might overcome tendencies to personalize what others say, procrastinate when action needs to be taken, or drive for perfection when "good enough" is almost always what is needed.

There is the fourth "watch-out" of busyness. In the spirit of slowing down to speed up, empowered leaders find the right balance and cadence of activity, and commit to the great law of management: it is *never* about time and *always* about priority. What does this mean for you, your beliefs, and your daily habits?

Eckhart Tolle, a leading teacher in consciousness, has said, The voice in your head is not who you are." While we must learn to trust our ourselves and our instincts, we must also take good care of our inner dialog. One of the most important practices for any leader is to monitor and soften your inner dialog to be more kind, friendly, and honest. How might you improve the quality of conversations that you have with yourself?

As you develop your leadership style, always be on the lookout for how your mind tells stories and deploys cognitive distortions. Similar to dealing with limiting beliefs and deceptive fears, good leaders avoid distortions such as mindreading, stereotyping, labeling, motivated reasoning, and all-or-nothing thinking.

You can develop healthy habits to replace limiting thoughts and behaviors with easy daily practices, just a few attentive minutes each day to change the nature of your thinking, being, and doing. Rather than use artificial force to be powerful, use inner wisdom to be empowered. Wisdom is the practical use of awareness, experience, and insight to help ensure the wellbeing of yourself, the enterprise, and those you serve.

In closing, there are a few timeless fundamentals of leadership we have explored in this book. Leaders evolve from a *me* to a *we* orientation. They know the paramount importance of values and culture, and reinforce them in both formal and informal interactions. Leaders create the conditions for people to do their best work and recognize and reward them for their contributions. They use true power based on mind, body, and spirit wellbeing, leading with an open mind, open hands, and open heart.

There are many ways to grow as a leader. Shed limiting beliefs and behaviors, develop your inner wisdom and true power, and view each day as a new opportunity. Life is full of chances and choices. Seek guidance, ask for help, and stay resilient. One thing is certain in an uncertain world, your path will be an amazing adventure.

Index

A-frame of actualization, 13
Business model, definition, 34
C-currents of consciousness, 94-95
Capability, enterprise, 35, 40-42, 73
Change and transformation, 44-48
Compassion, 13, 108
Consciousness, enterprise, 92-99
Consciousness, leadership, 94-99
Culture, conditions, 85, 87, 91, 92, 102, 124
Culture, definition, 101, 102
Customer acquisition, 29, 32, 40-42
Employee engagement, 85-87
Employee satisfaction, 85-87
Employee value proposition, 85-87
Empowerment, 1, 9, 10, 15, 18, 99, 104, 107, 109-111, 117, 118, 125
Entrepreneurial spirit, 42-44
Equanimity, 13, 17, 21-24

Intentional, integral, inspirational, impactful, 18-24
Knowledge work, 67-71
Law of management, 14, 127
Leadership communication, 113, 114, 115, 124
Leadership, competencies, 11-13
Leadership, executive, 123-126
Leadership, impact, 10, 11, 20, 118, 119, 124
Leadership, network, 74-76
Leadership, paradigm, 7, 8, 27, 51, 83, 104, 114-126
Leadership, proven practices, 10, 11, 123-126
Leadership, response frames, 100
Leadership, responsibilities, 9, 10, 117, 118, 126
Leadership, team development, 111-113, 125
Leadership, trust, 18-19
Mindsets, behaviors, practices, and abilities, 7, 8, 19-24, 91-95, 116-122, 127, 128

Performance management, 46, 47, 66, 67, 86-90, 99-101, 112
P-model of power, 108
Power, 15, 16, 107-110
Productivity, definition, 52, 54, 56-58
Productivity, improvement, 54, 55, 62-66, 68-70, 73, 74, 116, 117
Productivity, killers, 58, 59, 70
Productivity, proven practices, 59, 60
Self-actualization, 13, 18
Self-empowerment, 107-110
Self-limiting beliefs, 7, 14, 127, 128
Self-sabotage, 127
Strategy, definition, 34, 35
Strategy, execution, 44-48, 123, 124
Strategy, framework, 29-33, 40-42
Strategy, map, 38-40, 46
Value creation, activities, 22-24, 36, 37, 53-55, 124, 125
Value creation, definition, 56-58
Value creation, framework, 37
Value creation, metrics, 77-79
Value networks, 71-76
Wellness, health, 13, 20-24, 86, 107, 109, 126-128

About the Author

Chris Ellis has lived and worked in all regions of the country serving organizations and communities as a senior executive, strategy consultant, leadership advisor, professional coach, university educator, and volunteer mentor. He has collaborated with well over one hundred enterprises in many industries to improve strategy execution and value creation. His passion is to help leaders at all stages of their journey further develop inner wisdom for higher impact, greater meaning, and better living. Chris was educated at Northwestern University, the University of Chicago, and Duke University. He can be reached at wisdompathways123@gmail.com.

www.ingramcontent.com/pod-product-compliance
Lightning Source LLC
Chambersburg PA
CBHW070233180526
45158CB00001BA/468